THE POLITICAL THEORY
OF
ERIC VOEGELIN

Barry Cooper

Toronto Studies in Theology
Volume 27

The Edwin Mellen Press
Lewiston/Queenston

Library of Congress Cataloging-in-Publication Data

Cooper, Barry
  The Political Theory of Eric Voegelin.

  (Toronto studies in theology ; v. 27)
  Bibliography: p.
  Includes index.
  1. Voegelin, Eric, 1901-   --Contributions in
political science. 2. Political science--History--20th
century. I. Title. II. Series.
JC263.V632C66 1986   320'.092'4   86-23517
ISBN 0-88946-771-4 (alk. paper)

This is volume 27 in the continuing series
Toronto Studies in Theology
Volume 27 ISBN 0-88946-771-4
TST Series ISBN 0-88946-975-X

The Edwin Mellen Press   The Edwin Mellen Press
Box 450   Box 67
Lewiston, New York   Queenston, Ontario
USA 14092   L0S 1L0 CANADA

Printed in the United States of America

To

Jake, Bobsy, and Juicer
Hughes, Hank, and
Hungerford

ACKNOWLEDGEMENTS

I would like to thank Judi Powell, Martha Lee, Ann Griffiths, and Janet Harvie who attended to the boring mechanical aspects of producing a final copy. Janet Harvie also is responsible for the index, but not the bibliography. I am responsible for that and, vicariously, for the mistakes that Powell, Lee, Griffiths and Harvie probably made.

TABLE OF CONTENTS

PREFACE

Who is Eric Voegelin? It may seem strange that this question is still asked more than half a century after his thinking first came into print. The fact remains that his work is more esteemed than understood, more admired or categorized than studied. In a manuscript dating from 1945 and bearing the title, "Last Orientation," Voegelin explained the position of those men whom he called spiritual realists in times of confusion and disorder.

> If the realist would throw himself into the general melee as one of the contestants, he would defeat his philosophical purpose. In order to be heard he would have to become a partisan himself, and in order to become a partisan he would have to surrender the standards of rationality. If on the other hand he has sufficient spiritual strength as well as philosophical consciousness to take his position beyond the disorder of the age,...he will remain socially ineffective to the point of not even being understood.

Other spiritual realists to whom Voegelin made reference and who lived under analogous circumstances included Machiavelli, Bodin, Hobbes and Spinoza. Their characteristic insights into the spiritual disorder of the age separated them from it. Surely something akin to this has been Eric Voegelin's experience.

And yet, those who make the effort to study Voegelin's work, to consider his arguments reflectively, and attempt to understand him as he understood himself, gain the impression not so much of encountering a new political philosophy as of recognizing what they have been waiting for. This has certainly been my own experience.

There are other more systematically conceived introductions to Voegelin's political philosophy. The monographs by Sandoz and Webb, collections of critical essays by Sandoz and McKnight or by Kirby and Thompson are useful and they are recommended, as are the two collections published to mark his 60th and 80th birthdays.

The present collection was originally written over a period of years and was presented intermittently at several scholarly gatherings. The first four chapters have been published before in more or less recognizable form, but the language has been reworked to attempt to make it more consistent. The order is roughly chronological and proceeds from the more or less orthodox studies of political history and political texts to a brief exposition of some aspects of Voegelin's acount of consciousness. These essays should not be read as a systematic exposition of Voegelin's political philosophy. The genre into which the book falls is perhaps similar to what Marshall McLuhan used to call a probe. It is, of course, an unfinished exercise, as is political philosophy itself.

Herb Richardson, who has done much alone and with slim resources to bring Voegelin's work before the public, encouraged me to bring these pieces together, and I am grateful for his friendly support and engaging energy. Would that large and better endowed committees moved with a tenth his drive, because Voegelin's teaching is important not only for academics and the inhabitants of various asylums and gardens and towers. There is a certain urgency attached to the contemporary course of civilizational disintegration that may partially excuse the imperfections of the present collection. More practical readers may consider it a _livre_ _de_ _circonstance_ or a bulky pamphlet.

*

I have used what are becoming conventional abbreviations for Voegelin's works. Full bibliographic references are given in the Appendix.

Barry Cooper

Calgary

INTRODUCTION

Political science, as any science, is concerned, like the second part of the Organon, peri hermeneias, with the question of interpretation. It is not usual in the literature on hermeneutics to consider scientific discourse as also hermeneutic. Generally, a contrast is made between science and "hermeneutics." The consequence has been, to use the title of Gadamer's great study, a conflict between (hermeneutic) truth and (scientific) method.[1] This modern contrast dated from the Romantic era and owed its force to the widespread belief that the contemporary epoch was wholly and totally different, which was simply another way of saying that the past was seen to be strange, foreign, or alien. Two things may immediately be noted about modern hermeneutics: first, interpretation has tacitly been affirmed to be an historical enterprise, the recovery of a truth that once upon a time was clear, but now has become hidden; and second, interpretation has become chiefly the avoidance of misunderstanding rather than the art of understanding.

So far as the political, social, or human sciences are concerned, identifying the origins of hermeneutics with Romanticism is a vague approximation. First of all, there is no compelling reason to identify science with a Newtonian-scientific method, nor therefore, to identify hermeneutics with reaction to scientism. On the contrary, as Voegelin has said, if "the use of a method is made the criterion of science, then the meaning of science as a truthful account of the structure of reality, as the theoretical orientation of man in his world, and as the great instrument for man's understanding of his own position in the universe, is lost." Indeed, "the subordination of theoretical relevance to method perverts the meaning of science on principle" (NSP, 5-6). As a purely pragmatic matter, however, one cannot ignore the importance of Newtonian and Baconian scientific and technical knowledge nor the impact it has had upon political science or political philosophy. It remains to the credit of the nineteenth-century historians (whatever the deficiencies of historicity in other respects) that they insisted upon the fact that the knowing subject, including the political philosopher, was a part of what was studied. That is, one does not confront history, politics, society, etc., as one would confront a thing. One participates in the object of study; one is a part of a larger whole.

The fundamental participation of the political philosopher in the things studied lies at the root of what has been called the hermeneutical circle. Stated most broadly, a text, which includes, analogically, all meaningful action, cannot be understood except by understanding its context. This holds, for example, for a word: the meaning depends on the sentence of which it is a part; the sentence on the paragraph; the paragraph on the chapter; the chapter on the book; the book on the whole of the literary form concerned, and so on. That is, ultimately one's understanding of a part depends on one's understanding of the whole. But the whole is not a given that is prior to the individual element --in this example, the word.

Here, then, is the central paradox of interpretation: one must presume the unity of the many so as to designate them by a common name, and then use that name to define the unity of the many. First, the evidence must persuade the observer; it does the prescribing. And then one uses a concept as a norm on the basis of which evidence is to be included as relevant; now one's concept does the prescribing. Thus, one moves from experience or feeling of unity to postulated principles, and back to a critically reassigned unity.[2] The circularity of the argument is obvious. Since such arguments are never fully satisfying, attempts have been made to break the circle. Typically, this has been done in one of two ways. Following the terse formulation of Paul Ricoeur,[3] they are: first, reality is seen as a genuine appearance of meaning, or second, reality is seen as a mere show and truth lurks above, or beyond, or behind, what seems to be there. But neither strategy can be a complete success on its own. On the one hand, interpretation involves risk, the commitment to one thing and not another, but on the other hand, the manifold of reality is full of endless shadings, qualifications, and interpenetrations of phenomena, so that a simply true and univocal interpretation is impossible. Inevitably there exists in interpretation a mediation or translation of another historically separate or noneveryday experience into the present. To introduce these essays on Voegelin's political philosophy we begin with a description of the two interpretative styles.

*

Interpretation may be considered as recollection or restoration of a manifest meaning that is addressed to one personally as a commandment, proclamation, or message. For the recipient of such a meaning, misunderstanding is indistinguishable from disobedience. For the political philosopher reflecting upon this interpretative style, however, a certain analytical detachment is required. The first step, then, amounts to a phenomenological description of the object of meaning and of the animating intention that sees things that way. That is, the first step is to believe with the believer in the reality and truth of his words or action --but without any commitment to the absolute validity of the object of his belief. At most, one deals with a comparative context.

But second --and especially with texts in political philosophy that claim to tell a truth about human affairs generally, as distinct from texts that describe particular factual situations-- the question of absolute validity must be raised and faced. No 'one bothers to read a great text unless one expects to be addressed by it. This expectation presupposes a confidence in the language symbols used: one looks upon them first of all in terms of being addressed to human beings such as oneself and not as spoken by human beings and so possibly doubtful or wrong. One has confidence in the truth of symbols, that they fulfil their signifying intention by actually transmitting the intended meaning. Symbols have a persuasive force; but by acknowledging it one has already violated the initial phenomenological neutrality. This was inevitable insofar as the truth of something has been addressed to a human being; it has not, therefore, simply been made up by a scientific analyst. That is, one has been made to participate in the meaning of what is said because there was no other way it could be understood. The analogue from sense experience is hearing. One may not like what one hears, one may disregard what one hears, but the meaning of the message can not be in doubt, for, precisely on the basis of one's certainty that one has grasped it, does one respond by dislike or disobedience, by veneration, submission, or whatever. At this second stage, then, interpretation binds the symbol's giving of meaning to the intelligent initiative of consciousness.

An illustration of this level of interpretation is Voegelin's discussion of the myth of judgement at the close of Plato's Gorgias. In order properly to understand Plato's text, Voegelin showed, one must allow oneself to be persuaded by it. One must see that the dramatic contents of the text, the conflicts between Polus, or Gorgias, or Callicles with Socrates, in truth express the manifold experiences of one's own life. The alternative is, in effect, a choice of misunderstanding and therefore an act of disobedience. As Voegelin remarked: "In the symbolism of the myth, eternal condemnation of incurable souls is the correlate to the refusal of communication on the level of the myth of the soul; eternal condemnation means, in existential terms, self-excommunication."4

A third step is reflexive. The political philosopher commits himself to communication, to follow the initiatives of consciousness, because he is, in fact, concerned for the truth. And political philosophy is so concerned equally because of the inadequacy --that is, the untruth-- of already present, but empty, signs, formalized language, allegories, dogmas, and silence. One could say that, by rights, one expects the truth. In this respect, when the truth is not experienced, political philosophy becomes an act of resistance to untruth. Such resistance appears to us positively as an act of reminiscence, first of all as an historical re-collection.

The result, however, is a kind of non-result: there may be a progressive synthesis where each meaning is clarified by further images that are seen as more comprehensive, but equally any particular meaning may dissolve into more primitive elements. Since the presence of meaning depends upon one's commitment to truth rather than the specific formulation that is occasioned by one's commitment, every particular symbolization of truth will be followed, so to speak, by an afterthought that indicates the nonobjective status of the reality recalled to, and present in, consciousness. In Voegelin's formulation, truth is truth experienced, not a property of linguistic or other symbols. Accordingly, the meaning of symbols "can be understood only if they evoke, and through evocation reconstitute, the engendering reality in the listener or reader. The symbols exist in the world but their truth belongs to the nonexistent experience which by their means articulates itself."[5] The personal and material investments involved in the meditative reconstitution of the experience of nonexistent reality are further reasons why no interpretation can ever be final, as is

the nonobjective, nonexistent "content" of the reality
experienced.

*

A second interpretative strategy understands its
task to be disillusionment, a purging of the psyche.
Again there are three steps.

First, the primacy of the object is called into
doubt, and with it, the ability of the representation
to fulfil its meaning by incorporating the subject into
its truth. Meaning is seen to be a mysterious result
of culture or history, limited not by itself but by
method or perspectives that are themselves lacerated by
an economy of impulse, desire, and passion. The great
danger, therefore, is illusion, which is not an
epistemological category as is error, but is derived
from human desires. Consciousness may be tempted not
by disobedience but by emotional indulgence. And in
any case, consciousness is held to be dubious and
unreliable. Demystifiers are like radical Cartesians:
Descartes may have doubted that things are as they appear,
but he did not doubt that consciousness was as it appeared
to itself. Demystifiers do.

Secondly, however, the "school of suspicion" was
not simply destructive. Descartes doubted things in
order to make way for the indubitable and mathematical
truths of consciousness. Likewise his successors followed
their doubts about consciousness with an interpretation
or deciphering of the expressions of consciousness. If

consciousness is not what it thinks it is, the relation between what it is, and what it (falsely) thinks it is, must be accounted for. Here the fundamental relation is betwen what is latent and what is manifest. What we must do is replace the untrustworthy consciousness of meaning with a science that is irreducible to conscious- ness, and so avoids the untrustworthiness of it. One constructs a theory of illusion that shows consciousness to be false consciousness, a compensation for the hardness of life, a consolation, an opiate, an expression of one's spiritual disorder. And an opiate is needed, that is, falsely needed, because of the contingencies of cul- ture, history, alienation or self-alienation. Here the suspicious interpreter confronts those whom he takes to be men of guile. They reverse the works of falsification by their own practical science or technology of demystification. If the analogy from sense-experience in the first strategy was hearing, in the second one it is sight. There is no response to a call, but rather insight into the sense of a phenomenon. Once the insight has been gained, the illusion can be avoided.

Third, therefore, is the moment of return to trust. After suspecting the illusions of consciousness, and even if one can create a "second reality" and live one's life more or less according to it without being taken for a lunatic, even the fiercest, most inconoclastic demystifiers place some trust in consciousness. Even Marx, for example, wished so-called historical "necessities" to be understood. That is, the purpose of undergoing the hard discipline of reducing appearances to their psychological or sociological causes, of

explaining them by an account of their individual or
historical genesis, of analyzing their emotional or ideological function --the purpose of this reduction, suspicion, and destruction is to lay bare, and force one to
confront and to experience necessary reality.

The result, in Ricoeur's words, is "a clearing of
truthfulness in which the lies and ideals and idols,
are brought to light and their occult role in the strategy
of desire is unmasked."[6] The threshold of political
philosophy has been reached from this side with a call
for the destruction of idols. Now what? Two options
are apparent: to erect another idol and arbitrarily
declare it final, or to incorporate into the interpretation
a demystifying analysis of the analysis. That is, one
undertakes an analysis of consciousness, a discourse on
the origins of one's intellectual acts, at the same
time as one provides an analysis of the phenomena.

The first option is simply dogmatic and entails an
abandonment of the interpretative strategy. In this
respect it is an admission of irrationality. The second
consists in a reflexive modification of the second strategy
and a return to the first one, namely meditative
reenactment of experienced reality. To be more precise,
the two interpretative strategies are in fact complementary, though they are used for characteristically different
purposes. To state the question in a somewhat shocking
way, it is incumbent upon the political philosopher both
to meditate upon the truth of reality and to communicate
the meaning of his meditation to others by making that
meaning articulate in symbols, which is done by a strategy

of reminiscence, and it is incumbent upon him to expose and refute falsehood, for which an interpretative strategy of suspicion is most appropriate. This formulation of the obligations of the political philosopher should be only somewhat shocking however, because it is no more than a paraphrase of the opening chapter of the Summa Contra Gentiles of Thomas Aquinas. One purpose of the following essays is to indicate that Voegelin meets Thomas' criteria for a sapiens.

NOTES

1 Hans-Georg Gadamer, Truth and Method, (London, Sheed and Ward, 1975).

2 H. Jonas, Philosophical Essays: From Ancient Creed to Technological Man, (Toronto, Prentice Hall, 1974), 263.

3 See The Conflict of Interpretations: Essays in Hermeneutics, ed. D. Ihde, (Evanston, Northwestern University Press, 1974).

4 OH, III, 45, (emphasis added).

5 E. Voegelin, "Immortality: Experience and Symbol," 235-6.

6 P. Ricoeur, Freud and Philosophy: An Essay on Interpretation, tr. D. Savage (New Haven, Yale University Press, 1970), 230.

CHAPTER ONE

THE CRUCIBLE

Eric Voegelin was born in Cologne, January 3, 1901, the son of Otto Stefan Voegelin, a civil engineer, and Elizabeth Ruehl Voegelin. In 1910 the family removed to Vienna, where Eric Voegelin resided until he was forced to flee to Switzerland following the occupation of the country by the Nazis in 1938. He left because he was on a Nazi hit-list; he attained that honourable position chiefly as a result of his writing four books during the 1930s, the last and most polemical of which was The Political Religions. This chapter is concerned with presenting the background to Voegelin's later and more famous post-war work.

His secondary education in Vienna stressed modern languages, mathematics and science. In 1917, for example, he studied Einstein's new theory of relativity with his high-school teacher. Following the excitement of the Bolshevik Revolution, Voegelin read Marx's Capital and, until he studied first-year economics with Ludwig von Mises, considered himself a Marxist. In later life he was fond of saying that after he learned a little economics, Marxism ceased to be a problem.

When he entered the University of Vienna, Voegelin's interests were drawn to mathematics, to law, and to the new program in political science. He eventually chose the last because, he said, his enthusiasm for mathematics had waned and he was equally unexcited about the prospect of becoming a civil servant, which is what a law degree almost certainly would have meant. In addition, a political science degree could be earned in three years rather than the more usual four, a significant consideration owing to Voegelin's poverty. He completed his doctorate with Hans Kelsen and Othmar Spann in 1922. Kelsen was famous for having drafted the post-war Austrian constitution and as author of the "pure theory of law." Voegelin later introduced Kelsen's doctrine to the United States.1 Spann introduced Voegelin to the study of classical political philosophy and to the modern system-builders, Fichte, Hegel, and Schelling.

According to his long-time friend, Gregor Sebba, Vienna during their student days, a "shabby, sardonically cheerful city was an invigorating cultural center of the first order, teeming with talent, ideas, experiments, hospitable to every kind of intellectual venture from the stiffly orthodox to the wayward." It was still possible, Sebba said, "to bring together scholars and politically engaged people of every persuasion for informal debate on the burning current issues —probably the last group where Liberal and Marxist, Jew and antisemite, Socialist and Monarchist sat down together until civil war ended all that in 1934."2 The civil disturbances of 1934, as Voegelin later argued, made necessary the establishment of an "authoritarian state" as an attempt to protect Austrian society against ideological sectarian political movements.3 During this period Voegelin participated fully in the intellectual life of the city, attending the private seminars of Kelsen, Spann and von Mises, as well as the less formal Geistkreis to which

Sebba referred. This group met monthly to discuss a wide range of topics.

The appeal of Hans Kelsen for Voegelin lay in his analytical precision. Kelsen's drafting of the constitution, his court decisions, and his commentary on the constitution taught Voegelin the necessity of a careful and responsible reading of texts. The logical coherence of the legal system was supplied by the pure theory of law. In principle, Voegelin has maintained that double vision, of logical coherence and of careful and responsible fidelity to texts, throughout his own philosophical work. His disagreement with Kelsen came not over the theory of law but over the commitment by Kelsen to a neo-Kantian methodology that attempted to delimit the field of study by the method used in its explanation. This was a methodological shortcoming that Voegelin detected in much more obvious ways with Marxism, racist thinking, scientism, and any number of other ideological movements. Eventually, Voegelin disagreed with Kelsen over just this methodological point. Kelsen believed that the logic of the legal system defined the field of study of politics generally. Under pressure of events in 1934, Voegelin realized that political problems were more comprehensive than legal ones; that the law, as Madison wrote in The Federalist, Number 48, was but a parchment barrier in the absence of a genuine political community. As early as 1924, Voegelin published an essay contrasting the pure theory of law with the wider range of materials covered by the study of politics as practiced during the early nineteenth century.[4]

Othmar Spann was a more comprehensive scholar than was Kelsen. His importance for Voegelin's later life is twofold: first, he introduced Voegelin to the problems of classical philosophy. But second, and in some ways more significantly, Spann's romantic nationalism attracted a circle of romantically nationalist students. These people were important in a negative way, for some of them later became involved in the Nazi movement and in even more radical political movements opposed to the Nazis. During the mid- and late-1930s, Voegelin saw first-hand, in his former associates, the consequences of intellectual irrationality applied directly to political activism.

In 1922 Voegelin obtained a fellowship to attend summer school in Oxford. Officially he was there to improve his English. In addition, however, he was able to attend the lectures of Gilbert Murray, the distinguished British classicist. For a brilliant young man of twenty-one years, a summer in Oxford at the feet of Murray held the promise of expanding his intellectual horizons through contact with a civilized foreign culture.

Two years later he won an even greater opportunity for study, a Laura Spellman Rockefeller Fellowship, which took him to the United States for two years work at Columbia, Harvard, and Wisconsin. The importance of this first stay in the United States lay in the fact that Voegelin was forced to confront directly the larger world that lay beyond central Europe as well as the day-to-day problems of living in a vigorous democracy. Equally important, he escaped the recondite intellectual

disputes of Vienna. Under the tutelage of John Dewey
and Erwin Edman, Voegelin discovered English common sense
philosophy, eventually reading the works of Hamilton
and Reid.

Very briefly, the British "common sense philosophers"
argued that common sense was an attitude towards reality
that was equivalent to the attitude of the philosopher,
but without the linguistic sophistication or symbolic
luminousness used by the philosophers to express and
form their attitude. As Voegelin wrote much later in
Anamnesis, common sense "is the habit of judgement and
conduct of a man formed by ratio. One could say it was
the habit of an Aristotelean spoudaios without the luminos-
ity of knowledge of the ratio as the source of his
rational judgement and conduct."[5] The other side of
the common sense philosophers' teaching was that philosophy, chiefly classical and stoic philosophy, was an
analytically elaborate articulation of the common sense
attitude or experience. In his later works, this insight
regarding the relationship of attitude and sentiment
regarding reality, what he later called reality experienced, became a central pillar of his interpretative
enterprise. The first conclusion that Voegelin drew,
however, was political. Maintaining a continuous tradition of experiences, sentiments, attitudes and insights
of classical philosophy without the complicated discursive
trappings of sophisticated academic language contributed
much to the intellectual climate of opinion and to the
cohesion and public decency of a society. "Civilized
homo politicus," he wrote in Anamnesis, "need not be a
philosopher, but he must have common sense."[6] The example

of Anglo-American constitutional democracy was before him, a reality experienced.

Conversely, Voegelin recognized that the highly erudite and abstract language of German philosophy and German social science was empty of common sense. That too was reality experienced. The philosophical form remained, but the substance of the philosophical attitude towards the great political questions of justice and injustice, moderation and immoderation, statesmanship and irresponsibility, piety and impiety, was absent. This had, and still has, great and disastrous consequences for public decency in Germany. The difference between contemporary Germany and the Germany of sixty years ago, Voegelin has said, lies in the comparatively low intellectual stature of the contemporary positivists, neo-Hegelians, existentialists, Marxists and what-not who carry on these enthusiastic debates.

The first lesson he drew from his stay in the United States was that American society substantively enacted or lived out a philosophical tradition more comprehensive and meaningful than anything he had discovered in Europe. American pragmatism, as this common sense attitude has been called, was less articulate than the methodological environment of Germany, but by the same token, that is what enabled Americans to retain their sense of the concrete. Voegelin was impressed, for example, with Dewey's category of "likemindedness," a term used in the King James translation of the Bible to render the Greek term homonoia. And homonoia was a problem in classical and Christian philosophy about which a great deal had been written. Voegelin realized that Dewey was, in effect, working on the same problem, the problem of spiritual community, that classical and Christian thinkers had considered. This impressed him powerfully as evidence of the real or substantive continuity of the Western spiritual tradition in the United States.

The following year Voegelin left New York for Cambridge and Harvard. There he encountered Alfred North Whitehead, newly arrived from Cambridge, England. The second term of 1925-26 was spent at Wisconsin where Voegelin met John R. Commons, whose Human Nature and Property had been published the year before. Commons introduced Voegelin to the major themes of American government, especially the Supreme Court. A final Anglo-American influence on Voegelin during his stay in the United States was George Santayana, whom he studied at the suggestion of Erwin Edman. Santayana's scepticism was the perfect complement to the common sense of Dewey and the metaphysical questioning of Whitehead. Santayana was immensely learned, like Voegelin's European teachers, but completely uninterested in the dogmatic squabbles of neo-Kantians.

In 1928 Voegelin's first book, On the Form of the American Spirit, appeared. The five chapters reflected the several topics he studied during his stay. The first, on time and existence, synthesized his studies of English and Scottish common sense, Hodgson's philosophy of consciousness, the speculations of James and Peirce on time, contingency, and "radical empiricism." Implicit, and sometimes explicit, was a comparison of these

Anglo-American thinkers with the German theory of "internal time-consciousness" represented by the phenomenology of Husserl. A second chapter was devoted to Santayana; the third to Puritan mysticism, chiefly represented by Jonathan Edwards. Chapter Four, some fifty pages in length, was concerned with the Anglo-American analytical theory of law. The two parts, on British and American variations in the theory of law, were compared to the pure theory of Kelsen. A final chapter was on John R. Commons.

The book is important both for understanding the intellectual development of Voegelin and as one of several accounts of America written by foreigners. We would like to emphasize its first aspect. For two years Voegelin was living in an environment where the level of sheer intelligence and brain-power was equal to that he had known in Vienna, but the concerns of the people he met had nothing at all to do with the heretofore important questions of methodological polemic. Instead of considering the merits of the Marburg versus the Southwest German School of neo-Kantians, Americans were concerned with the act of political foundation and the implications of the American founding through the political and legal culture represented by the founding fathers, by Lincoln, by the decisions of the Supreme Court. The background of Christianity and classical culture as a living reality informed the discussion of the great American political institutions. None of this was present in Europe. What Voegelin discovered, upon reflection, was that there could be, as William James indicated, a plurality of worlds. Consciousness of plurality, and specifically of the difference in substance and in form between the highly articulate intellectual culture of central Europe and the substantive common sense of America was captured in the closing words of Voegelin's book, in a quotation from Commons:

> I do not see why there is not as much idealism of its kind in breeding a perfect animal or a Wisconsin No. 7 ear of corn, or in devising an absolutely exact instrument for measuring a thousand cubic feet of gas, or for measuring exactly the amount of butter or casein in milk, as there is in chipping out a Venus de Milo or erecting a Parthenon.... Of course, a cow is just a cow, and can never become a Winged Victory. But within her field of human endeavour she is capable of approaching an ideal. And, more than that, she is an ideal that every farmer and farmer's boy --the despised slaves and helots of Greece-- can aspire to.[7]

The immediate effect of his exposure to America was that Voegelin was innoculated from the intellectual and ideological extravagance that attended such events as the publication of Heidegger's famous book, Being and Time.

Voegelin's priorities had changed: what was most important was reality experienced, not the debates derived or removed from reality, to say nothing of debates whose relationship to reality was tenuous or nonexistent. The longer term effect was that this insight concerning plurality was transformed into an interpretative strategy: the plurality of lived experiences express the plurality of human possibilities, which in turn may be realized in a plurality of political forms and civilizations.

The third year of his fellowship allowed Voegelin to study in France. As with his time in the United States, Voegelin was again immersed in the real-life problems of cultural and intellectual pluralism. He read widely among the symbolist poets and Valery; he worked his way through the great literature of the eighteenth and nineteenth centuries, discovering on the way that the French history of consciousness runs parallel in some respects with the English and American. Bergson's great work, The Two Sources of Morality and Religion, which was to have considerable impact on Voegelin's later work, had not yet been published, though Voegelin read Bergson's earlier studies. In addition he was attracted to French memoirs, a genre that began in the seventeenth century. Finally, Voegelin plunged into the literature of the French moralists. It is probably fair to say that his time in Paris resulted in less dramatic changes than did his time in the United States. One insight, at least, was reinforced: the study of literature, and especially of poetry, is study of the self-articulation of language. That is, Voegelin's French studies emphasized again the importance of the self-interpretation in the study of meaning. Throughout his writing, Voegelin has consistently maintained that one must retain a strict fidelity to what in 1928 he called "self-speaking phenomena," and what later were termed symbolisms. One does so by paying close attention to meanings as they are understood from the inside or imaginatively. Voegelin agreed with the interpretative canon of his great contemporary in political philosophy, Leo Strauss: one must strive to undertand an author as he understood himself. The shock of America and Voegelin's response to it, his overcoming of central European provincialism without succumbing to American provincialism, brought this home to him in everyday life. It was confirmed by his reading the culturally more familiar French writers.

The experience of America awakened in Voegelin an awareness of the limitations of the central European intellectual culture that had nourished him. At the same time it enabled him to understand the greatness of those who devoted their lives to resisting what he later called ideological swindles. Among these scholars was Max Weber. Weber had a lasting influence on Voegelin in three areas. First, Weber's long essays of 1904-5 on Marx and Marxism destroyed whatever pretension to science that Marxists could conceivably claim. Weber's analysis showed, very simply, that Marx's writing was untenable ideology. Weber, in short, taught Voegelin a more radical criticism than the implicit rejection of Marxism that the study of economics entailed. The study of economics was equivalent to common sense insofar as it showed why no responsible economist could be a Marxist. In addition, Weber indicated the sources of the refusal by Marxists of responsibility and of common sense. Their ideological commitments The ideological commitments of Marxists eclipsed their common sense and their sense of responsibility. This act of overcoming became a central focus of Voegelin's later analyses of ideological con-sciousness.

Second, Weber's distinction between the "ethics of intention" and the "ethics of responsibility" contained the genuine and permanent insight that the unforseen consequences of moralistic action are the responsibility of the actor. This insight, which could be formulated in commonsensical terms as well, was important because it was developed in opposition to the ideological position that if one cherished certain "values" with great conviction, the "sincerity" with which they were held and the morally elevated intentions that one made public would be sufficient to excuse any suffering that might be caused by trying to put them into action. Weber's distinction made it clear that the "values" that are assumed to be so morally elevating are scientifically invalid ideological inventions. It was to protect his science from ideological infection that Weber developed his famous "value-free" method of inquiry devoted to the analysis of cause-and-effect relations in the process of society. The great defect with this method of analysis, as Voegelin pointed out later in The New Science of Politics, was that the criteria by which materials were accumulated for analysis as well as the reasons for an ethics of responsibility were themselves identified as "value-judgements" and thereby outside the boundaries of scientific or rational analysis (NSP, 13-22). What saved Weber from relativism was, apparently, his personal mysticism: Weber experienced reality though he was unable to account for it. So far as political philosophy was concerned, this was not entirely satisfactory; after all, students and other readers wish to know the reasons why an ethics of responsibility, for example, is, politically or prudentially speaking, superior to an ethics of intention. Moreover, when the rational order of existence is excluded in principle, passions are likely to move you to embrace the high moralism of elevated ends in which considerations of means are eclipsed; this is a recipe for ideological fanaticism.

The third area in which Max Weber, among others, was a model for Voegelin, was in the range of his scholarship. With his usual bluntness, Voegelin remarked that Weber established once and for all that one cannot be a successful scholar in the field of social and political science unless one knows what one is talking about. In this regard Weber, with his knowledge not only of modern civilization but of ancient and medieval civilization, of Near Eastern and Far Eastern civilization, and of India, remains an inspiration. Without this command of the empirical materials, Voegelin said, once cannot call oneself a scientist or comparativist.

In addition to Weber, the great classical scholar Eduard Meyer and the circle around Stefan George produced works during the late 1920s and 1930s that served to shape the intellectual climate influencing Voegelin. And finally, the literary influence of Karl Kraus should be mentioned. For ten years before his death in 1937, Kraus defended the language of Goethe against the corruption of the journalists, the publicists, and the extraordinary vulgarity of the politicians. His equivalent in English would be someone such as George Orwell or Richard Weaver. As with Weber's insistence on comparative knowledge for an empirical scientist, Kraus and George taught that restoring shape and dignity to language meant a recovery of the subject matter expressed by language, a recovery of meaning, and thereby of the full amplitude of reality experienced. A concern with language is part of the resistance against ideological nonsense inasmuch as ideologies seek to destroy not language but the consciousness of reality expressed through language, and to substitute for it a derived language expressive of the alienation from reality by the ideologue.

From the foregoing remarks it is clear that by the early 1930s Eric Voegelin was a superbly trained young scholar. Not only had he undertaken the usual academic exercises, but he had travelled widely and, more importantly, his travels had actually had the effect that travel is supposed to have: it broadened his understanding rather than confirmed his prejudices. His experience in America had innoculated him forever against the temptations of high-sounding abstractions just as Weber's ethical teaching had taught him the importance of political responsibility, prudence, and that consequences mattered in judging the justice of political action. In the language of classical philosophy, his psyche was well ordered. The times, however, were anything but well ordered. Voegelin's four books of the 1930s were all concerned with the political catastrophe that was about to occur, or rather, that had already begun and was to engulf the world within a few years.

*

"The motivations of my work are simple," Voegelin has said, "they arise from the political situation. Anybody who lives in the twentieth century, as I did,

with an awake consciousness ever since the end of the
First World War, finds himself hemmed in, if not oppressed,
from all sides by a flood of ideological language, meaning
language symbols which pretend to be concepts but in
fact are unanalyzed topoi".[8] Voegelin's approach to
the study of political phenomena, including the phenomena
aggregated into crises, was radically personal. This
has led some critics, even sympathetic ones, to detect
a degree of arrogance in Voegelin's work. This is a
misinterpretation. Voegelin insisted that his work arose
from experience, the real experience of political disorder. By clarifying the nature and extent of that disorder,
he would indicate its common dimensions. That is,
Voegelin's interpretations were anything but
ideosyncratic. He began with common sense and common
experience and attempted to persuade through an appeal
to his readers to experience imaginatively the meaning
he experienced concretely. That procedure, it seems to
me, is hardly evidence of arrogance. If anything, it
indicated Voegelin's concern with "likemindedness."

A major aftershock in the continuing political crisis
of Western political life occurred on the periphery of
Western civilization, in Russia. The Bolshevik revolution
was undertaken by men who said they were Marxists. The
interpretative principle that instructs the political
philosopher to begin with the self-interpretation of
individuals and of events indicated that the work of
Marx would be central to a serious understanding of the
new Bolshevik regime, a regime whose most obvious and
novel characteristic was the practice of large scale,
state-directed murder. The study of Marx and of the

first regime inspired by Marx's teaching ensured that the general problem of ideology would be a central topic of analysis. The second, and not unrelated political event that sharpened Voegelin's concern with ideology was the rise of Fascism and National Socialism. These were collective political disasters, not personal tragedies or regrettable errors; the appropriate attitude of a political scientist under such circumstances was to resist the growth of these ideologies through an analysis of the fraudulent language and constricted experience of their practitioners. Voegelin undertook this resistance the way philosophers do, by careful analysis, by exegesis, and by thought and judgement.

In 1933, the year Adolf Hitler became chancellor of the German Reich, Voegelin published two books on race, Race and State and The Intellectual History of the Race Idea. The first book analysed the pretensions of the "race idea" to scientific legitimacy. It did so by submitting the biological, anthropological and ethnographic claims of this "idea" to analysis and systematic exposition. In a sense, by undertaking a "scientific" study of the claims to science of this "idea" Voegelin was conducting a magnificent parody. Many readers of this book have wondered how Voegelin was able to maintain his detachment, sine ira et studio. In part, Voegelin may have wanted to fool the Nazi censors; it is more likely, however, that he followed the methodological procedure indicated earlier. If the race "theorists" consider their doctrine to be science, then, he may have said, let us compare it with the findings of biology. When it is found not to accord with biological science, let us account for this error in methodological terms, as a "mistake" in what he then called the "primordial manner of seeing." A careful reader of the introduction to this study, where concepts such as "primordial manner of seeing" were introduced, would soon discover that Voegelin was, in fact, concerned with spiritual disorder. The background to Voegelin's understanding of biology was acquired during his stay at Columbia when he became friends with a number of young biologists, including Kurt Stern who was at work on genetics theory using the famous fruit fly. As Max Weber taught, Voegelin knew what he was talking about.

The second book, The Intellectual History of the Race Idea, was one of Voegelin's best. It began with the words: "The knowledge of man has come to grief," and went on to explain that evidence for this grief was to be found in the current state of "race theory" as "inauthentic thinking." The key to the inauthenticity of thought, more fundamental than the deformations of scientific biology, was the denial of the Greek and Christian conception of human existence as a unity of body and soul. Accordingly, no scientistic reduction of human existence to its genetic or other immanent or material constituents could achieve anything but the destruction of social and political order. Voegelin undertook a lengthy critical analysis of the genealogy of the race "idea" and showed its convergence with other ideological systems, notably liberalism and Marxism. In any event, the Nazi race "theories" rested not upon experience, since there was no biological or ethnological basis for the notion or race, but upon a dogmatic superstition that Voegelin identified with a perversion of natural science. Coupled to scientistic superstitions was a twisted millenarianism that transformed the Germans into salvific carriers of the Nordic Idea, and Jews into the diabolical "anti-idea." The combination of scientism and millenarianism had the logical implication that the triumph of the Nordic Idea required the physical extermination of the bearers of the material that constituted the Jewish "anti-idea." Here was a recipe for mass murder. Voegelin's account of the implications of the Nazi "idea" was one of the most accurate of contemporary reports. For that reason, perhaps, it was widely overlooked or disbelieved.

In March 1933, the Austrian government declared that Parliament had eliminated itself and that a new "authoritarian" regime had established itself. Three years later Voegelin published a book analyzing the new regime. The first part of the book is an analysis of the terms "total" and "authoritarian." These terms were not theoretical concepts but political symbols that served to express the assumption of a collective entity ruled by a state institution that was itself governed by whomever happened to represent the collectivity. The second part of the book surveyed the problem of constitutionality in Austria since the establishment of the Dual Monarchy in 1848. What makes this material currently topical is the argument that modern nations and states are "totalities" ruled by "authoritarian" regimes. Voegelin was the first to point out the implications of this language when it is used in political analysis.

The existence of a body politic is a complex reality based on a large number of impermanent ethnic, ideological, economic, religious, historical etc. factors. When new regimes are created, as was the Austrian regime of 1933, by revolutionary fiat, their viability will depend not upon the legality of the foundation, since they establish new legal foundations, but upon the degree to which they are able to create a stable body politic through the experience of participation in a genuine political community. It was apparently Voegelin's view that the "authoritarian state," with all its shortcomings as a political body, nevertheless was able to defend Austria against the ideological radicalism of left and right. It might serve, therefore as a chrysalis within which a political community might develop. In the event, the annexation of Austria by the Nazis and the inaction by the Western powers put an end to these expectations. In the third part of the book Voegelin made a detailed analysis of Kelsen's "pure theory" of law and its connection to Austrian politics. Or rather, he showed that Kelsen's legal theory was inadequate to the properly scientific understanding of political reality.

The last of Voegelin's four books written in response to the political crisis of the 1930s was The Political Religions. It appeared in the spring of 1938 just in time to be confiscated by the invading Nazis. As with his postwar use of the term "gnosticism," Voegelin later expressed reservations over his use of the term "religion" to describe an ideological movement. The terminology was not simply wrong so much as vague and undiscriminating. The great change between this book and its predecessors, which may well reflect both the growing intensity of the political crisis and the growing awareness by Voegelin of the depth of the disaster that was about to occur, was the increasing sharpness of his rhetoric. Ideologies now appeared as spiritual diseases whose origins lay in the late middle ages when sectarian religious movements grew too powerful to be publicly suppressed as heresies. With the decapitation of God during the Enlightenment and His proclaimed murder during the nineteenth century, ersatz and immanent "political religions" were invented to express the deformed emotions and sentiments that once were expressed through Christian worship. In place of divine transfiguration through grace in death, humans sought to transfigure themselves into perfect men or supermen. The central argument of the book, which expressed a fundamental truth adequately enough, was that ideologies were by and large anti-Christian religious movements.

Certain subsidiary themes have lost none of their validity. The inadequacy of most critical analyses of ideological movements is a consequence of the dogmatic commitments of most contemporary intellectuals. The raising of questions of spirituality is rigorously excluded by positivists, Marxists, Freudians, and of course progressivist liberals. But if ideology is a spiritual disease, their analyses are bound to be misleading. To state the question more aggressively, one might say that they are accomplices in their own destruction. If "metaphysics" has become a term of abuse and religious commitment an "illusion" whose future demise is to be anticipated with scientific satisfaction by psychoanalysts, one is not left with many insightful diagnostic instruments.

Despite the soberness of Voegelin's analysis, despite the implications contained in the epigraph to the book, namely the first words above the gate to Dante's Inferno, despite the lament of the Epilogue for the innocent about to perish, despite the failure of this book to comprehend the demonic evil of the age, despite, indeed, the human ability to flood the world with sufficient foulness to obscure the God who sustains it, men still cannot alter the structure of existence. When God is eclipsed by ideological dogma, the world supplies its own ersatz gods; when the symbols that express the human search for the divine source of justice and being are destroyed, world-immanent symbols that express human alienation from the divine ground are developed in their place. The analysis of the deformed symbols and the varieties of alienation, no less than the exegesis of symbols that express the plurality of ways by which the structure of existence is expressed and made articulate, were the twin tasks of the new science of politics that Voegelin developed after the war.

Voegelin did his greatest work in the United States. His multivolume history of political ideas, his most famous book, The New Science of Politics, and his magnum opus, Order and History, were all written in America. It was in America, moreover, that he found the initial spiritual difference that enabled him to begin his long and difficult task of restoring to political science its proper grandeur as a science of human experiences of order. The four books on ideology, written under the pressure of strenuous events, constitute the necessary initial and negative moment, the exposure of the lie.

The following two chapters are devoted to a consideration of the major philosophical and methodological themes of Voegelin's History of Western Political Ideas. The early volumes may be most profitably seen as an analysis of the genesis, nature, and disintegration of Western civil theology. The later volumes, of which a fragment has been published under the title, From Enlightenment to Revolution, amount to an account of the growth of Western spiritual irrationality, what he was to call the eclipse of reality. These are severe and sweeping terms comparable in force to the great divisions made by Plato, Augustine or Bodin. It is a measure of Voegelin's greatness that his use of them is fully adequate to the crisis he experienced, diagnosed and described. The genesis of his work, to paraphrase what has already been quoted, lay in the political situation of the twentieth century and the ideological language used to describe it. For Voegelin and for political philosophers, that language expressed but did not account for the crisis.

NOTES

---

[1] See Voegelin, "Kelsen's Pure Theory of Law." Full bibliographic information is given in the Appendix.

[2] Sebba, "Prelude and Variations on the Theme of Eric Voegelin," in Ellis Sandoz, ed., Eric Voegelin's Thought: A Critical Appraisal, (Durham, Duke University Press, 1982), 7

[3] Der Autoritaere Staat, (Vienna, Springer, 1936)

[4] "Reine Rechtslehere und Staatslehre"

[5] Anamnesis, 353

[6] Anamnesis, 353

[7] Voegelin, Ueber die Form des Amerikanischen Geistes, (Tuebingen, Mohr, 1928), 237-8

[8] This quotation is taken from a series of tape-recorded autobiographical reflections. A copy of the typed transcript is in the Institute for Political Science in Munich. My thanks go to Professor Peter Opitz for kindly allowing me access to this document. These reflections are reproduced in extenso in Ellis Sandoz, The Voegelinian Revolution: A Biographical Introduction (Baton Rouge, Louisiana State University Press, 1981).

CHAPTER TWO

WESTERN CIVIL THEOLOGIES

Extensive work on contemporary civil religion in the United States allows one to assume with confidence that political scientists and theologians are familiar not only with the reality but with the concept. An extended prelude is therefore not required. Voegelin's description of the genesis and significance of the concept is most widely available in The New Science of Politics. His analysis of various western civil theologies is found in The New Science, in Order and History, in From Enlightenment to Revolution,[1] in the manuscript of his History of Western Political Ideas, and in several widely scattered articles.[2] Even though a lengthy introduction is unnecessary, because of the later development of Voegelin's thought, particularly with respect to history,[3] a few summary remarks on the nature of the topic may be in order.

As the source references given above indicate, much of Voegelin's discussion of civil theology was written prior to the appearance of Order and History. Many other articles dealt with contemporary difficulties of life in modern industrial society. In this category the prewar books may be located. It is also true, of course, that the term "difficulty" is hardly adequate to describe the murderous activities of the totalitarians. The discussion that ended with The Political Religions was continued after the war under altered circumstances.

So far as these works are concerned there are no major interpretative difficulties. There Voegelin simply presented an analysis of the meaning and limitation of contemporary civil theologies, of the minimal requirement for a just polity, of the position of the philosopher with regard to modern civil theologies, and so on. Nevertheless, it is also true that, after the appearance of Order and History the incidence of his theoretical use of the term declined. Now, it is certainly true that Voegelin discussed the topic in connection with Plato in Volume III, for example, that the term is used in Volume IV, or that a minimum of interpretative ingenuity is required to discover a civil theology of Israel and of the Near Eastern empires. To do so, one first must formulate a concept or definition and proceed to examine the evidence in light of it. Then one proceeds chronologically to analyze the changes and continuities, within the single conceptual type.

The procedure just outlined is approximately that advocated by Voegelin in 1944.[4] At that time, Voegelin argued that political philosophy combined in a single discourse a narrative account of political history and a conceptual analysis of political "ideas." That is, political philosophy or political science included both an account of what human beings have done to one another and an account of what they thought their doings signified, what meaning they gave to it all.

The methodological assumption governing this approach was that the history of political philosophy is not an autonomous enterprise, but rather is subordinate

to the actual empirical structure of political history.
One assumes, in adopting this procedure (as we shall do
in the present chapter), that there is a structure to
political history, a meaningful configuration of events
that lends itself to theoretical analysis. The discovery
of meanings <u>in</u> historical changes is not, of course,
the same as declaring the meaning <u>of</u> history.[5] Nor,
one may add, is it a matter of historicism: not all
meanings and patterns of meaning are equally valuable,
nor are they assumed simply to represent the historically
contingent climate of opinion. By means of what, in
The New Science, Voegelin called "critical clarification,"
one can distinguish the truth represented by a political
society from that of a political philosopher.[6] Nevertheless, there remain certain methodological ambiguities
that may easily be obscured by the flow of the argument.
Specifically, the problem of equivalence of experience
and symbolization, which challenges the assumption that
history, as an order of succession, is serially structured,
is subordinated to the assumption of continuity.[7] That
this approach was methodologically defective is beyond
doubt; Voegelin's own arguments have shown it. It has,
however, the pragmatic advantage of being a first approximation, requiring few strenuous exegetical efforts.

The term theology is a Platonic neologism. In the
Republic (379a1-6, 382b7-11), Adeimantus wondered how
one could speak rightly of the gods when poetic and
sophistic speech about them was unacceptable. Indeed,
Plato called that speech a lie, and saw in the consequences
of "living a lie" the destruction of public order. In
the Laws (885a7ff), the hints of the Republic were more

specific: philosophers were charged with formulating doctrines or dogmas that expressed adequately their own spiritual insights, but in such a way that the nonphilosophers, who were a great majority, could understand, and in understanding live well, and thereby preserve the right order of the polis. From its beginning, then, the term theology had a public and political significance. As for the term gods, one may be permitted the use of a modern expression, such as ultimate reality or object of ultimate concern, to indicate approximately its meaning.

Let us specify the problem more precisely. Unless there were agreement about what was real or true, which included agreement about the gods, it was said, the city would not endure. In Plato's time, evidently, there was no agreement about these things: some said the gods did not exist, others that if they did, they were absent or had emigrated or did not really care for humans anyhow, and still others that, although they did care for humans and for justice amongst them, it was more to the point that they could be bribed with sacrifices.[8] Whether anyone really believed such things is less important than that many acted as if they believed them. The result was clear in Adeimantus's bewilderment: the gods did not constitute a limit beyond which humans may not pass. In effect, there were no limits, no real limits, to what men could do. There were, of course, so-called limits, conventional limits, but no one was obliged or could be forced to respect them. This, for Plato, was the lie; his writing ought be seen, in this respect, as an attempt to tell the truth because of the evil political consequences of human action undertaken on the basis of the lie. That is, we approach the present topic, civil theology, by emphasizing resistance to the lie rather than attraction to truth.

In opposition to the lie Plato proposed his own counter-dogma: the gods exist; they care for humans and their justice; they cannot be bribed. One corollary, at least, was clear: justice is good for humans and, because the gods care for mankind, they strive to ensure that justice be done. This means, as Plato said in the Gorgias, that, while it is best neither to do nor suffer injustice, it is, if this be the sole choice, better to suffer than to do evil, and worst of all is to do evil with impunity (OH, III, 26ff). The inevitable suffering that comes to the body politic as a whole when it is unjustly governed (whatever the governing part may get away with, and for however long a time) would seem to be met (OH, III, 36 ff; OH, II, 373). Injustice that is never punished is apparently impossible. The basis for this and other complementary Platonic doctrines is to be found in the experience of reality, or of the gods, that the philosopher undergoes.

In The New Science, Voegelin referred to this experience under the head of anthropological truth, and contrasted it with an antecedent cosmological truth as well as with the lie. By cosmological truth was meant first, the self-understanding of a political society, that its existence expressed the meaning of the cosmos, and second, the commonsensical observation that, if a political society was to exist at all, it must be some sort of cosmos, order, and not chaos, disorder. Yet, it could not be just any kind of order, at least not for one such as Plato. In Voegelin's words, "A political society in existence will have to be an ordered cosmion, but not at the price of man; it should be not only a microcosmos but also a macroanthropos" (NSP, 61). That is to say, in practice, one finds a clash of truths. On the one side, the truth of the given social order, or rather, the self-understanding of those who live it, and on the other, the bringer of the new truth. With Plato, a fitting contrast was provided by Pericles who, in his famous funeral oration, went so far as to call acknowledged criminals good, agathon, solely by reason of their service to the city. Goodness, it seemed, was what served the city, where service was determined by men such as Pericles. Yet, the ruin of Athens showed that service to the goals that Pericles sought was not simply good. It would seem, on the evidence of Thucydides as well as of Plato, that the Athenian cosmion was corroded by the lie.

It does not follow from this, however, that anthropological truth can ever find a suitable political incarnation. Indeed, neither Plato nor Aristotle saw any likelihood of a good polis ever coming into being but that it would immediately commence to disintegrate (OH, III, 121ff, 350ff). But then, if philosophical experience can serve solely as a critical instrument, one wonders what positive political significance it may have. That is, if all that the philosopher, the incarnation of anthropological truth, can do is explain why men like Pericles lead their cities to glory and disaster, surely this constitutes no greater insight than the cosmological wisdom that informs how the things that are created also perish.

Two things may be said in reply. The first, quite simply, is that while no city may ever rightly be called good or just, it does not follow that goodness or justice has no reality at all. There may be a good man even in the midst of a city that is less than good; alternatively, it may be that goodness is a nonexistent reality, a reality that appears only in a vision but that is itself outside, or beyond, or transcendent to, the individual who experiences the vision, the noesis, to use Plato's term. We will not consider these difficult matters here, because it is the second point that is more important for our discussion.[9]

It is undeniably true that the language of Platonic philosophy is heavily dependent upon political imagery. At the same time, the meaning of this language and imagery, that is, Plato's argument or discourse, indicated a trans-political reality accessible to a properly trained and desiring psyche. And that reality experienced within that sort of psyche was the actual standard on the basis of which the political norms and practices of the day, along with the beliefs of citizens concerning them, were to be measured. The philosopher was the measure of the polis, Plato said, because the god was the measure of his psyche (Laws, 716c). The real experience for which the imagery of measurement was the symbolic articulation, the experience of being under a judgement much more meaningful than the rise and fall of cities, was the

source of the philosopher's authority and the basis upon
which he raised his own truth in opposition to the truth
of the city (OH, III, 254, 263). Indeed, the persecutions
of the city could only confirm, for example, Socrates's
contention that it was better to suffer than to do injustice.

At the same time, the unhappy end of Socrates raised
the issue of social effectiveness. Were the alternatives
only death or flight? Not necessarily; but only because
the question was badly put. The conflict between the
city and the philosopher and between their respective
understandings of the highest realities was and is a
conflict of meanings, or myths, or interpretations.
Victory in the conflict between the myth of the polis
and the myth of the psyche was gained by the latter.
Institutionalized in the several academies, porches, and
gardens that survived in Athens after it had long since
ceased to be a polis, after it had attained the status
of something like a provincial university town, philosophy
still bore a message of truth. The civil theology of
the Socratic psyche, then, still serves as a standard
by which the measure of contemporary political myths
can be taken. Only the terminological conservatism of
political philosophy, whose vocabulary is so closely
linked to polis life, misleads one into thinking that
the philosopher's civil theology is also bound to the
polis (OH, III, 293).

*

Voegelin's famous account of modern civil theologies
and their gnostic spirituality, to which we shall turn

presently, relied on many of the insights of classical philosophy. But modern civil theologies did not grow up in opposition to Plato and Aristotle. On the contrary, the moderns made use of the Greeks in their disputes with the prevailing orthodoxies of the middle ages. We must, therefore, give a brief account of the new truth of Christianity, its experiential basis, linguistic expression, and historical institutionalization. However crude and unsubtle the approach may be in other respects, political science is obliged to treat the Christian symbolism no differently than the Platonic. To do so, another beginning is required.

Droysen's great history of Alexander, published in 1883, was the first to emphasize the epochal decisiveness of the break initiated by the western invasion of Asia in 334. The age of Hellenic poleis facing oriental empires was extinguished, and what Voegelin called the age of ecumenic empires had begun (OH, IV, 153ff). Henceforth the distinction between Greek and barbarian had no immediate political meaning. When Athens, Sparta, Corinth, Argos, Thebes were just towns, Aristotle's notion, that by nature human beings were polis-beings, or that the good life could be lived only in a polis, was not very convincing. The compact ethnic unity of citizen, of polites, and polis split into a radical apolitical individualism on one side and on the other a cosmopolitanism that would have been quite foreign to any classical, fifth-century Hellene. The polis no longer gave a sense of purpose and place to human action and neither, it seemed, did much else. Alexander's conquests, and those of his successors, including the Romans, had vastly expanded the horizon of the ancient world, but in so doing they had disrupted its material basis and created a kind of spiritual vacuum. The new power organizations had made the political disorder of the Athenian empire, as described by both Thucydides and Plato, the common heritage of the Mediterranean basin. Whatever order existed was imposed from above, often by the stern arm of the military bureaucrat.

The great account of these developments was written by Polybius. In his work one sees for the first time a fundamental and coherently argued shift away from the persistent theme of Greek political philosophy, namely the internal structure of political units, or of the "best regime," to a topic more in accord with his experience of reality, namely the rise and fall of political units, whatever their internal structure (OH, IV, 117ff). The old question of justice and injustice within a polis no longer made sense when there were no political communities to speak of, or when sheer force of arms could pulverize them into a hapless collection of individuals. What mattered was the movement of power across the world: history, not the natural order, was the proper category of political analysis.

The dialectics of imperial expansion are familiar enough to us: when a political community expands and extends its rule over foreigners, it as well as the foreigners are changed. Exigencies of imperial rule draw forth an elite of power-brokers, cut off from popular culture and wholly devoted to an indefinite expansion; those who directly suffer the destruction of their community, as well as those who destroy their own community by destroying others, begin to reflect on the senselessness of it all. As an example of the first there are the famous apocalyptic visions of Daniel; and of the second, the work of Polybius himself, especially his account, preserved by Appian, of the victorious Scipio weeping in his hour of triumph over Carthage, in 146.

Polybius said that he wrote for "the common intelligence of mankind" (Histories, VI: 5,2). In Cicero one finds the perfection of his audience. A brilliant forensic orator and a lawyer untroubled by ambiguities, it is no wonder that generations of school children have learned their Latin at his feet. And yet, reading Cicero in search of an understanding of either empirical or of spiritual reality invariably is disappointing. As Voegelin observed, for Cicero that the Roman order is simply best, is the self-evident condition for debate. Anyone, Voegelin said, "who can speak of philosophy as a 'foreign learning,' to be respected but nevertheless to be considered as a spice that will add perfection to superiority, has, one may safely say, understood neither the nature of the spiritual revolution that found its expression in philosophy nor the nature of its universal claim upon man" (NSP, 90-1). For Cicero, the question of the best regime was simply not a problem. Accordingly, there was no concern, as there had been for the Hellenic philosophers, for questions of defective actualization of the idea of the best polis nor of the spiritual realities experienced in the psyche of the philosopher by which the polis and its order was measured. Nor was he troubled, as had been Polybius, with the world-historic senselessness of ecumenic expansion. The best regime happened to be the Roman. Nothing more need be said. It is perhaps fitting that one so sublimely indifferent to commonsensical observation should end with his head on a pike, at the sight of which, Plutarch said, the Romans shuddered for they saw there not the dead senator but the promise of things to come.

The victory of Octavian over Anthony was greeted not with dirges, lamentations and outbursts of anxiety, but by Virgil's second announcement of the advent of the Golden Age. The Aeneid was not a celebration of Rome, the polis, nor of the virtues of Romans, but of Rome the organized imperium with the Julian house at its head. By joining the story of the Trojan descent of the Julians, stemming from Aeneas, son of Venus, to the imagery of the Golden Age initiated by the victory of the Roman West over the Hellenized East, Virgil finally legitimized the upstart barbarians by showing they were really Greeks. The cost however could not be avoided: imperial Rome had lost its own tradition. Sooner or later even Romans could not avoid facing the fact.

So far as the question of civil theology is concerned, Virgil's myth hardly touched the still-present reality expressed in Scipio's tears. A Caesarian world ruler, a golden saviour such as Augustus, expressed but did not fulfill the hope of political redemption. Nor did anyone else. First of all, late pagan philosophy emphasized the meaningfulness of nature independent of political society. Moral autonomy and spiritual self-sufficiency, which constituted the good life, could be gained by and large only through ignoring power and politics. The mystery religions emphasized human dependence, not autonomy, and the need for divine aid in gaining purification needed for a good life. But here too, independence from political activity, or rather, indifference to politics, was stressed. Daniel's eschatalogical pattern of world history, when combined with the imagery of the suffering servant in Deutero-Isaiah, proved more promising.[10] Then the historical suffering of Yahweh's servant, Israel, could be transfigured into the public redemption of mankind.

In this context, the political significance of Christianity seems clear: it created, within an eschatalogically tense Judea and a Roman-Hellenistic world deprived of spiritual meaning but aware that epochal events were unfolding, a new community, a spiritual ecumene (OH, IV, 134ff). The relationship between the new ecumene and the equally ecumenic power organization of Rome was complex. Its decisive political feature seemed to be this: since any attempt to re-establish independent political communities would be crushed by Roman power, the actual coexistence of the several nations within the empire could serve as instances of a universal human meaning beyond the contingencies of power. But this innovation raised as many problems as it solved.

The spiritual meaning of the new community began, of course, with the personality of Jesus, with his power to heal or cleanse those who believed in Him, especially the poor in spirit. One can see the political problem by raising the question: was Jesus the Israelite Messiah?

According to Israelite expectations, the Messiah was a
royal warrior who would smite the foes of Yahweh's people;
the fate of Jesus however, looked more like that of the
suffering servant, which must have caused considerable
confusion for those of his followers who saw Him as
Messiah.   Their confusion was evidently dispelled by
the vision of resurrection,[11] which henceforth constituted
the fundamental evocative act of the Christian community.

The details of Voegelin's account are beyond our
immediate and more restricted purpose. Consider the
options: if Jesus were an Israelite Messiah, He was a
dismal failure; if He were a prophet He might have become
something like the Buddha. Instead there developed a
community under the leadership of an historical person
who was also the manifestation of divinity. But if
Jesus's presence were required for that manifestation,
His death would have meant its extinction. Instead,
the community substance was found in the spirit of the
resurrected Christ, the presence of which could be attested
only by visionary experiences of it. For political science, historical accuracy on this point is as irrelevant
as the endocrine processes and blood-sugar levels of
those who saw. What counts is that a new community was,
in fact, constituted on the basis of several visionary
experiences, whatever their genesis may have been and
however controversial their significance remains. On
the evidence of Acts 2, it would seem that the membership
of this new community expected the Christ of their visions
to be rather more active than he was. In fact, He was
supposed to bring an end to the world.

In the event, He did not. The community must again have been disappointed or affected in some other way, as they transformed themselves from a group living in keen anticipation of the end of days, from an eschatalogical community, into what Voegelin called, following Dempf and Troeltsch, an apocalyptic community (NSP, 108). The most elaborate statement of what this entailed is contained in the Epistle to the Hebrews. One gained membership in this new community, symbolized as communion with the Holy Spirit, by what may be called a change in personality. Secondly, unlike Danielic imagery, the foundation of the community was historically decisive; unlike Polybian fatality, membership in it, as result of individual spiritual change, was personally meaningful. A third important political feature was that the community was a compromise with the world. It was not a self-sufficient ethnic group, but a community governed by a spiritual law graven on the hearts of believers. Nor was it a sect of saints: all human beings were united in one mystical body, one community of spirit, though each had an individual place according to the mystery of grace.

Social relations were governed by the Israelite ten commandments, to which appropriation Paul added his own two-part summary; one must love God, and love one's neighbour as oneself. The direction of this teaching, when considered politically, was decidedly nonconsequentialist. Paul's admonition to the slavish brethren, that they were to love their masters because, and not despite, their masters' Christianity, revealed that some of the members of the community confounded spiritual freedom and political liberty. This did not mean Paul was dishing out opiates to the masses but that social status was a concern of this ecumene and not of much importance as compared to spiritual renovation (cf. I Tim., 6, 2). Hence, authorities were ordained of God with the limited and provisional task of using power against evil doers.

One may summarize this early Christian civil theology as outlined above under three points: (1) the different spiritual gifts within the one mystical body politic prevented Christians from turning themselves into a spiritual aristocracy so that potentially all persons could become members of the community; (2) recognition of the legitimacy of existing social structure made Christianity compatible with any social order; (3) the integration of government authority with the dispensation of God made it compatible with any political government. If one may use Voegelin's later vocabulary, the above three points may be said to represent the universalist political content of Christianity.[12] At the same time, however, that universalism was incarnate in a particular community, albeit one that understood itself as having an ecumenic mission. Our concern is not with the very subtle question of the relationship between Christian spiritual universalism and the putatively ecumenic Christian religion, but with the relationship of the new community, with its ecumenic aspirations, to the "nations," the ethne or gentes.

Within the community of Christians, the Jewish-Christian Jerusalemites, under the leadership of

James, brother of Jesus, demanded adherence to the Mosaic Law as a condition of entry. Paul opposed this ethnic or tribal particularism as being too exclusive, just as he opposed exuberant individualism in the form of glossolalia by insisting on rules to translate pneumatically inspired gibberish into articulate discourse (<u>OH</u>, IV, 244-245). Other difficulties involved regional, ethnic, personal, domestic and civilizational factors whose complexity makes a clear and distinct account virtually impossible. The result, however, was unambiguous: the community split into several churches, Nestorian, Monophysite, Orthodox. Furthermore, the political structure of the new communities was novel: they were missionary organizations, not poleis, nor military colonies, nor states. The intention was to unify the power organization of the Empire with the ecclesiastical organization of the missionary movement. This was never completely successful though it reached a high point under Constantine (cf. <u>NSP</u>, 97ff), after which St. Augustine's civil theology changed the terms of the discussion, effectively ending the debates of the Roman-Christian period.

*

The life and work of Augustine, a veritable <u>Summa</u> of his age, laid the foundations for western Christian political philosophy. The brief account here presented is confined to three topics: the question of civil theology proper, the question of history, which trenches upon the first, and the question of the <u>gentes</u>. As we shall see below, the modern anti-Christian civil theologies oppose the Augustinian on all three points as well as the Hellenic and Roman-Christian positions already outlined.

The term, civil theology, owes its preservation to Augustine who, in the course of his great polemic, The City of God Against the Pagans, adopted in a modified form the classification of Varro (cf. NSP, 80ff). According to Varro, civil theology was distinct from mythical theology, which was the discourse of poets who appealed directly to the multitude in a more or less magical way, as well as from physical or natural theology, the specialized discourse of philosophers, which was of no political significance. Civil theology, as was noted in connection with Plato, was the official religious teaching of the city; in Augustine's time it was akin to the mythical in being polytheist, but also akin to the natural in not being magical. Augstine's argument against Varro was, first, that the Roman civil theology was simply untrue. Now, if Varro were indeed a philosopher, that is, a proponent of natural theology, the objection was idle, since the whole purpose of civil theology is to be useful. Augustine's second objection, then, was precisely that it was not useful, least of all in securing the agreement of Christians who, by the fifth century, were numerous enough to cause a lot of political mischief (DCD VI: 5ff). But that was hardly an argument at all. It did, however, indicate the context of debate: "The Christian protagonists in this struggle were not concerned with the salvation of pagan souls; they were engaged in a political struggle about the public cult of the Empire" (NSP, 86-7).

The actual content of Christian civil theology was indicated by the title of Augustine's most famous book. "Two types of love constitute the two cities: love of self even to contempt of God constitutes the earthly, love of God even to contempt of self, the heavenly. Therefore the one glories in itself, the other in the Lord. For the one seeks glory before men; to the other, the highest glory is God who knows the conscience of men. In the one the rulers as well as the subjected gentes are possessed by the libido dominandi; in the other there is a mutual service of love, on the part of the magistrates through counsel, on the part of the people through obedience" (DCD, XIV: 28). There are clear echoes of Plato's eros as well as Aristotle's philia, the bond of the polis that ensures good counsel and obedience. And, of course, the symbol of the city was derived from Hellenic as well as Roman experience. Two features, however, constitute significant innovations.

The first was Augustine's construction of world history. Ever since the Epistle to the Hebrews this had been a central topic of Christian political speculation. The epochal significance of Christ had introduced a new question: whereas Hellenic and Roman thinkers were concerned with the mythic course of a single and particular people, Christians were concerned with the history of the world of mankind. Augustine's theory reworked existing symbols based on the six days of creation, the succession of generations from Adam to Christ, and the six phases of human life so as to bind together in a meaningful unity God, Christ, and mankind. The weak point in the symbolism was indicated by the imbalance in the number of predecessors to Christ or the number of phases of human life prior to the last one where, by analogy, mankind presently dwells. After Christ, the history of the world had no structure, no internal aim, until at some unknown point Christ would come again, like a thief in the night. For individual Christians, this was not too much of a bother: one could serve Christ by caring for the poor in spirit just about anytime. For communities it was less satisfactory, since it seemed to imply that the future entailed no constructive collective purpose (cf. DCD XIX). Under the conditions of the fifth century, or perhaps the present one, this attitude may be acceptable; at other times it would be rejected as fatalistic, defeatist, evasive, duplicitous, and evidence only of a scandalous loss of nerve.

However one wished to characterize the spiritual ambiguities and lacunae of Augustine's historical speculations, what was beyond dispute was that the world had been radically and uncompromisingly de-divinized (NSP, 100ff). Meaningful history was sacred history, the history of the city of God; the rest was profane. Generally it was no more than a dreary tale of treachery, lust, conquest and murder; occasionally a Socrates or Plato would relieve the gloom (DCD, VIII: 3-5) or Roman virtues of courage and republican liberty would receive their due (DCD, V: 22). On the whole, however, the secular world, simply by being distinguished as secular, could not contain the higher vision of perfection introduced by Christianity. The Church alone could mediate between sacred and profane history insofar as it represented

(but did not constitute) the heavenly city. Nothing,
therefore, guaranteed any of its members heavenly citizenship. Nor did political office simply mean earthly citizenship and final damnation. Augustine's achievement,
furthermore, reopened a series of political problems
that had been obscured by the Ciceronean complacency
adverted to above. In contrast to Cicero's abstract
legal definition of a people, Augustine said they were
"a group of rational beings bound together by a common
agreement concerning the things that they love" (DCD,
XIX: 24). By determining the concrete objects of a
people's love one could judge the quality of a common-
wealth: the heroic virtues of the Roman republic became
no more than its resplendent vices. Even if misdirected,
Roman courage was not of itself a vice, and Rome gained
its proper reward, dominion of the ecumene. And that
was all. Augustine was not, however, a clerk seething
with ressentiment; he took genuine pleasure in recounting
the glorious deeds of Scipio and Scaevola, but added
that Christ eclipsed them all. After Christ there could
be no additional pagan heroes, only martyrs. For a
millennium, Augustine's devastating indictment of pagan
civil theology overshadowed all pagan virtues.

Augustine's discussion of the gentes deserves special
mention. Ever since Alexander's time, the place of the
nations had been a problem. Cicero's solution, that
ethnic particularism was obliterated in the homogenizing
cosmopolitanism of Roman law, was theoretically invalid,
no more than an ex post facto rationalization of the
power of Roman arms. Moreover, the early church fathers
saw the existence of national individuality as a distur-

bance. Augustine acknowledged the legitimacy of the claims of national communities to individual existence: they were spiritual entities that ought be lifted to the level of Christian spirituality, not crushed out of existence.

Finally, one must mention an important omission: Augustine said nothing of the history of the gentes outside the Israelite-Christian symbolic orbit (cf. NSP, 109-110). Unfortunately for the pretence to universality, however, there existed Parthian and Sassanian dynasties in Persia. One solution was to create parallel histories. But this was not entirely satisfactory because, for example, both the Western Christian and the Parthian claimed to be histories of the world. How could there be two worlds? It was more convenient to forget about eastern history. The reality of eastern power, however, did not so easily disappear. Consequently, the image of the east became blurred; it was a mysterious place, vaguely a threat.[13] An alternative, first used by Augustine's pupil Orosius, and used for the last time by Bodin, was to integrate profane history within the four quarters of the cosmos. The usual pattern, however, was to subordinate profane events to a single straight line of meaningful time, to create an historiogenetic myth as Voegelin later called the procedure.[14]

This result had far-reaching consequences for medieval as well as post-medieval political thought. When, for example, the gentes appeared in force, as they did on the occasion of Augustine's writing The City of God, and succeed in doing away with the fourth Danielic kingdom, did the fifth monarchy, the kingdom of God, get established? Certainly not. Neither did the invader impose his own ethnic history on the defeated: rather, the Romanocentric story was continued, punctuated with "upheavals" and "disturbances." Orosius, for example, called Atalf the Visigoth, the "restorer" of Rome when he was quite clearly its destroyer. Likewise, the Germanic kingdoms were quick to appropriate Roman symbolism as their own, stressing thereby that their imperium was a worthy and legitimate heir to the earlier civilizational grandeur.

*

Augustine's civil theology was institutionalized in the evocation of the sacrum imperium (NSP, 108-110). The migration events and their aftermath ensured that the actual existence of a sacred empire as a power organization would be a long time in coming. Not until the reign of Henry VI (1190-97), when Germany, Italy and Sicily were under imperial control, when Richard held England in fief from the Emperor, and when the marriage of Henry's brother Philip to the daughter of the Byzantine emperor Isaac II gave him a claim on the east, can it be said to have had territorial existence. Even then, most imperial claims were contested and unenforceable anyhow.

Apart from determining the ethnic stock of western Europe, the migrations had the equally momentous consequence of destroying the civilizational area of the ancient world and establishing a new one, geographically situated on the outskirts of the old (cf. NSP, 45ff). As a result of its isolation, western political speculation became extraordinarily complex, an amalgam of Roman-Greek tradition preserved in the monastic and imperial foundations, of Greek philosophy mediated by Arabic transmission, of Jewish stories and scripture, of indigenous experiences linked to the growth of towns in the later middle ages, of autochthonic memories, of the diffusion of Arabic, Mongol, and Turkish civilization, and so on. Such complexity ensures that practically any statement made about the middle ages will invite qualification and occasion dispute. Nevertheless, a few general comments may be offered.

The papacy and the Frankish kingdom only gradually withdrew from the sphere of Roman power centred in the east. By the same process they drew together to form the new Carolingian Empire. During the pontificate of Gelasius I (492-6) were forged the first systematic statements of the correct relation of spiritual to temporal power, his famous doctrine of the two swords.[15] Not until the turn of the sixth century, under Gregory the Great (590-604) was it possible to give even a semblance of form to Gelasius's doctrine, and it took another century and a half before the relations between the Church of St. Peter and the Frankish kingdom were clear. Finally, the great event of Christmas, 800, the coronation of Charlemagne, established the multi-national imperial institution whose image dominated the remaining centuries of medieval political history. The one Christian community, its spiritual centre in Italy, its temporal centre north of the Alps, had found, at least in theory, its Gelasian embodiment.

In practice things were not so neat. Papal real estate and regal paraphernalia, such as palaces, titles, dignities and pomp, on the one side were balanced by oaths of loyalty to the monarch that bound those who swore them to holy service. The sheer power and personal charismatic authority of the Germanic kings was reduced by their dependence on Church personnel for administrative staff and by the spiritual plenitude of the pope. The dramatic high point in settling the overlapping jurisdictions was, of course, the investiture conflict, culminating in the spectacular event of Henry IV standing repentant in the snow at Canossa.

At the same time that the Gelasian civil theology reached its apogee, medieval spiritual politics were being transformed. The monastic foundations, the papal and episcopal reforms, the new spirituality of the crusades, and the military and mendicant orders, revealed a self-assertiveness whose intramundane consequences eventually undermined the Augustinian basis of the sacrum imperium. As early as 1100, the anonymous author of the York Tracts seemed to be able to live perfectly well as a Christian without benefit of Gelasian civil theology and the institutional mediation of Church and Empire. He was far more than a controversialist, however, because his argument concerning the present age touched the core of Augustine's teaching. For the Anonymous, the present world was intrinsically interesting, not just a waiting for the end, a holding pen, a mere prelude to real posthumous action.

To express this novel sentiment he reworked Pauline and Augustinian patterns of divine history. In place of the six-day pattern with its unlimited last day of waiting, the Anonymous constructed a pattern of three ages during which the realm of God attained its fullness on earth. In the first, which was that of the Old Testament, one finds a prefiguration of priesthood and kingship. In the second, the age of the New Testament, which extended from the first to the second coming of Christ, one finds the true priesthood of believers and the true priesthood and true kingship of Christ. And the third and final age was the true realm of God, when believers would reign as kings in glory, as Christ did during the second age.

Let us consider some of the implications of this startlingly new speculation on the spiritual history of mankind: Redemption was no longer simply a willful act of divine grace but a step leading to the ultimate kingship of man; Christ, king from eternity, adopted the human form of priest only to make humans potential co-rulers of all reality by redeeming them; accordingly, the royal was superior to the priestly function because it corresponded to the divine nature of Christ while the other corresponded to the human. Perhaps most interesting of all, if Christians became true priests during the second age by means of their participation in the mystical body of Christ, this could mean only that the priests of the Church were illegitimate usurpers. Once upon a time they were needed to combat schism and heresy, the Anonymous said, but no longer. Now, they have become a hindrance. What is more, they were foreign and un-English;

if the papacy wished to instruct people, the Anonymous roundly declared, let them visit pagans. In western Christendom they were superfluous and certainly had nothing to teach him about the meaning of Scripture. Here, clearly was a person for whom the Gelasian dispensation was a dead letter. His arguments and objections presage the subsequent dissolution of the medieval evocation of the sacred empire.

The Anonymous was not simply an isolated thinker, a brilliant inhabitant of a remote corner of a remote northern kingdom: he was symptomatic of a new complex of sentiments and a new self-understanding. In the two centuries following the Investiture Conflict one finds a large number of individuals who saw the Gelasian symbolism as inadequate and imperial organization as foreign or outmoded. Not surprisingly, most of them, like the Anonymous, lived on the fringes of the imperial heartland: John of Salisbury in Norman England (NSP, 184-5), Joachim of Flora in Calabria (NSP, 110-13), the Emperor Frederick II and St. Thomas in Norman Sicily, and Siger in Brabant.[16] Each of these men experienced the meaning of the world in a way that was not exhausted by the Augustinian saeculum senescens. The growth of a new sentiment of a saeculum renascens, meant that the distinction between this world and the realm not of this world was weakening: this world was gaining legitimate status within the saeculum of Christ.

It is a commonplace to observe that innovation is accompanied by interpretation. When late medieval human beings understood their actions as innovative, the question of what the new experiences meant naturally arose. Moreover, the novelties had to be placed in a context and related to other events, prior, contemporary, and envisaged. The Anonymous of York, for example, was a particularly conscientious interpreter. His symoblism of the three ages bypassed the Gelasian civil theology entirely to strike directly at its speculative Augustinian core. With the new age, there began the process of political self-interpretation, a process that is far from exhausted even today.

Two aspects of this process ought be clarified at the outset. First, the people who undertake the interpretation of the new realities will be likely to see their own place as decisive in shaping the new order. They may conceive their function as being confined to as narrow a theatre as their local community or it may expand to a group of communities, to the western world, or to the whole of mankind. But secondly, so long as they remained within what we banally call the Christian tradition, there existed one absolute limit: the new age was only an innovation with regard to the mundane order of things. Yet, the irruption of wordly forces, even within the one overarching Christian _saeculum_, posed particularly grave problems for civil theology. Owing to its unsystematic nature, the temptation to throw out the substance of Christian spirituality along with its obsolete formular trappings was increased.

For political science, the disintegration of the _sacrum imperium_ as an evocative symbolism introduced three systematic problems. First, is the question of who actually undertook the actions whose result was the new age. Here the emperor Frederick II is the prime representative of an _individual_ political personality who put his mark on an era; the Church, especially under Innocent III, or later, Norman England, serve as representatives of _communities_ organized as wordly agents (NSP, 38ff). Second, these agents of change sought to impress upon the age the meaning they experienced in their own existence. The most notable expression of this spirit was in the monasteries: monastic life, for Joachim of Flora, the most significant discussant of the topic, represented the spirit of the third and final age (NSP, 110ff). Third, the rules according to which the new forces acted were made increasingly explicit. The initial form this attention to the world took was juridical, but it was later expanded to include a concern with operations of power, pure and simple. The first two questions are central to our topic; the third, associated with the reviled names of Machiavelli, Bodin and Hobbes, is of great importance for political science as a whole. Historically, the topics overlapped and their implications were worked out haphazardly. Accordingly, the following enumeration of persons and events does even less justice to the rich texture of empirical reality than has been done elsewhere in this chapter.

Following Voegelin, we have said the new age was characterized by the entrance of intramundane worldly realities into the context of a Christian spirituality whose major orientation had always been towards a transcendent beyond. Merely to list the major teachings of the main figures who appeared during the period between the conclusion of the Investiture Conflict, with the Concordat of Worms, 1122, and the era of St. Thomas, a century or so later, indicates the direction and magnitude of the change.

The _Policraticus_ of John of Salisbury (1159), possibly the only text of medieval political philosophy that has an immediate appeal for contemporary undergraduates, is most important for concentrating on "political man" as the appropriate unit of investigation, leaving the ones "whose hearts are cleansed" out of the picture. His famous doctrine of tyrannicide, which gave the individual the right to use his own judgment in political matters, even to the point of executing a ruler, revealed as well that the individual was the source of the new intramundane sentiments.

With Joachim of Flora the new sentiments reached the stage of reflective consciousness and the structure of the age as a whole became topical. The result of Joachim's speculations, as even the most casual reader of _The New Science of Politics_ must learn, was the postulation of a new dispensation. The specific contents were less important than the significance of the fact itself, that a new image of human being was being evoked: the new realm would be peopled by a spiritual elite unencumbered by the social, political, or ecclesiastic forms of the dying age. The spiritual branch of the followers of St. Francis saw themselves as that elite; St. Francis's own teaching of brotherly love was equally revolutionary in that it made of ordinary laypersons a spiritual order equal in dignity to the feudal and ecclesiastic ranks of the day. His letters "to all the faithful" presumed a status equal to that of pope or emperor; his attacks on the world in the name of evangelical poverty and of imitation of the life of Jesus had the effect of exalting creaturely existence and suffering so that Christ ceased to be the head of a differentiated Christendom but was constrained to symbolize the conformance of a particularist group. As if to balance the Franciscan glorification of the poor and humble who are everyone's servants, Frederick II, stupor mundi, identified himself with the Christ of Easter, not Good Friday.[17] His praise of Jesi, his birthplace, as a new Bethlehem, his self-identification as the Joachite leader of the third age, as true ecumenic emperor, adored by land, sea and air, friend of peace, patron of charity, founder of law, preserver of justice, moderator of the cosmos, and so forth, was further evidence that the reconciling symbolism of Christ as both suffering and triumphant had split along the lines of social hierarchy.

A final figure in this picture gallery was Siger de Brabant, the first person who can properly be called a philosopher in the modern sense, that is, one whose understanding of philosophical life was dissociated from theology and who claimed historical authority solely on the basis of his speculative intellect.[18] With Siger one finds the pathos of an intramundane intellectual that is as vehement as the intramundane individualism of John of Salisbury, the historical personality of Joachim, the intramundane Christianity of St. Francis, or the intramundane rulership of Frederick.

In all cases one finds a pattern of mutual support
between their experience of existence and the accounts
they rendered of it: immanent existence is part of the
immanent structure of the world which is proved by the
revelation of it through an intramundane intellectual
activity. Correspondingly, a new mystical body politic
was evoked as the carrier and embodiment of the new
meaning; a new ethical teaching, generally of a utilitarian
type, was created in order to promote the interest of
the intramundane community. In short, the disintegration
of medieval Christianity was well underway. Intramundane
spiritual forces, embodied in individuals and particular
groups, had in an increasingly public way broken the
power of the old evocation. The decidedly modern direction
in which the new civil theologies developed calls for
scarcely any elaboration.[19]

Only with St. Thomas, whom Dean Swift did not
hesitate to number among the moderns in the famous querelle
des anciens et des modernes, does one find a balance
between the vast historic changes of the world and Christian spirituality. New and revolutionary bodies politic,
constitutionally organized peoples, bourgeois commercial
society, the natural prince, the independence of the
intellect, all these novelties, which in others led to
excess, exaggerated militancy, heterodoxy, and even
anti-Christian sentiments, were in Thomas's personality
harmonized with Christian universalism. Like his grand
relation Frederick, Thomas was highly sensitive to the
forces of the day, but he far surpassed the emperor in
spiritual qualities; like John of Salisbury, he had a
humanist's interest in characters, but he also saw a

place for a Christian political man; his spiritual individualism was equal to that of St. Francis, but he did
not go overboard in his evocation of a community of the
spiritually free, for he also recognized the proper function of the prince; Joachim's epochal consciousness was
expanded beyond the horizon of monastic brotherhoods to
an ecumenic and imperial vision of Christian political
communities. In short, Thomas was the grandiose representative of politically, spiritually, and intellectually
mature Western man. His achievement became, so to speak,
a permanent acquisition of post-medieval political science. In our own century, for example, his arguments
have been invoked as the grounds for Roman Catholic
and, occasionally, Anglican civil theologies. But these
have been essentially rearguard actions: as Voegelin
remarked, "what is needed for the present is a new Thomas,
not a neo-Thomist" (ER, 22).

With St. Thomas one finds a political theorist
who combined encyclopedic knowledge, maximal spiritual
sensitivity, and intellectual brilliance. In principle,
he was a standard by which his successors might well be
measured. Because human existence is also historical,
however, his work could not be invoked in detail without
his being transformed into a dogmatic authority that
would bear increasingly less resemblance to empirical
events, existing institutions, and concrete experiences
of human beings. We have devoted sufficient attention
to the details of Voegelin's discussion of the growth
of western civil theologies to its most adequate, and
at the same time historically limited, form that only a
few brief remarks concerning the regression to contempo-

rary modernity need be made. We will discuss a late stage of the disintegration in the next chapter.

*

A word of caution is in order to guard against misunderstandings. To assert that Thomas provided the most adequate historical embodiment of modern western Christian civil theology is to court the risk of being dismissed as a Thomist. This is a mistake. Thomas may have been modern but he is not contemporary. The range of his historical knowledge and systematic insight was great, but much has happened since his day. Thomas may yet be the common teacher of the Roman Catholic Church but that organization is in fact catholic only in aspiration. If one attends to the significance of one of Voegelin's most important aphorisms, that the order of history emerges from the history of order,[20] then it is clear that one must understand Thomas's successors on their own terms. One must seek to learn from them as well as his predecessors. In short, one must take seriously Voegelin's remark quoted earlier; indeed, one may go further: a new Thomas could not possibly be a neo-Thomist. More likely he would be one such as Voegelin himself.

However that may be, western civil theologies that attempted to replace those of Christianity or of classical antiquity can be briefly characterized as an imbalance that takes the form of endowing either nature or history, or both, with demonic and magical significance. Voegelin has given a detailed analysis of this problem in terms of its experiential motivation and symbolic result under the head of gnosis.[21] So far as the present topic is concerned, the growth of national states as meaningful political bodies in succession to the <u>sacrum imperium</u> is the most important pragmatic factor in understanding post-medieval civil theologies.

No less than five types of civil theology may be distinguished within the modern world.[22] First, are the successors to the Gelasian doctrine of the two swords. The earliest distinctive variation of the dualist structure is the Averroist version of Dante. The two heads, Emperor and Philosopher were to replace the prior duality of Emperor and the Pope. A later attempt to establish a mystical version was made by Bodin. This time the two heads were to be the National Sovereign and the Mystic-philosopher. Finally there are the host of ideological civil theologies, ranging from the Comtean division between Industrial Managers and Positivist Intellectuals to Leninist models of Toilers and the Vanguard. All of these versions have attempted to adapt the Gelasian division between temporal and spiritual to changed historical circumstances, consisting chiefly of new philosophical idioms, the new political bodies, and the development of ideologies.

A second general type is the minimum dogma.[23] In response to the wars of dogmatic religion, philosophers such as Spinoza (and, less explicitly, Bodin and Hobbes) attempted to formulate a basic creed that everybody would agree upon. Beyond this minimum, people could believe what they wished, so long as it did not come into confict with what was by law established. The nonminimalists would include the philosophical devotees of a life of reason as well as more exotic cultists.

Third are the sectarian activists who would impose peace by exterminating nonbelief, if necessary by exterminating nonbelievers. The chief examples are the several waves of revolutionary fanatics, beginning with the Puritans of the seventeenth century and extending to the Communists and National Socialists of the twentieth.[24] There is, however, an inherent contradiction within these kinds of civil theology insofar as their murderous activities tend to provoke resistance either from within the national polity in the form of civil war or else from without in the form of the international and then "world" wars. The imposition of an immanentist, sectarian state cult seems to be self-defeating in that it does not appear to be able to achieve the sought-for goal of civil peace.

A fourth general type is Lockean Civil Government. According to Locke, there is a naturally political realm, which alone deserves public representation, and then there is "religion." Religion is inherently or naturally private, a matter of personal conscience or individual taste. In fact, Locke's view corresponded only to the beliefs of moderate Protestants and Anglicans. Accordingly, his apparent tolerance of all kinds of private cults, again including the life of reason, was balanced by an intolerance of anyone who insisted upon gaining a public status for their religious beliefs.[25]

Lastly, there is the civil theology derived from Lockean doctrine, pluralist constitutionalism. This civil theology, a veritable orthodoxy among contemporary political scientists, assumes in Ciceronean fashion that the constitution is beyond debate: it is fixed, final, and best, to be subjected with difficulty to formal amendment, and open to interpretative modification by small increments at the hands of a skilled college of learned individuals. Under the over-arching umbrella of constitutional form, free rein is given to peaceful intellectual, spiritual, and pneumatic movements, cults, churches, ideologies and, once again, philosophy or the life of reason.

One may conclude that the contemporary political world is a field of competing civil theologies. It has often been maintained by Voegelin's detractors that he lumped together under the heading of gnosticism all that is modern. This is not wholly misleading provided one distinguishes between what is modern and what is contemporary. For, while it is true that modern gnosticism, in several typical variants is an innovation that historically succeeded the medieval-Christian, it has succeeded in obliterating Christianity no more successfully than Christianity obliterated the Socratic myth of the psyche. It did, however, contribute to the construction of our present ecumenic political, economic, and spiritual order. Furthermore, it is often said of Voegelin's argument about gnosticism that it is archaic, abstract, or simply arbitrary and fantastic. In reply it is maintained that, if one is to understand the miseries as well as the grandeur of the modern present, one must take one's bearings from a premodern source. Modern gnosticism is so intoxicating, the argument goes, that sobriety can come only from the classics or from medieval Christianity. One can certainly sympathize with such sentiments, but one may also be permitted to doubt their soundness. After all, we do not live in poleis, nor a sacrum imperium, nor, at least since the French Revolution, can it unequivocally be maintained that we live in national states (it has never been true for North Americans). An adequate contemporary civil theology would have to reflect the pragmatic contingencies of our present common life: ecumenic public and private bureaucratic organizations, mass political and religious movements, nuclear weapons and power stations, space exploration, medicare, and so forth, as well as the full amplitude of human spirituality. In closing, we can give but a few hints as to what such a doctrine would involve.[26]

The problem, in its stark simplicity, is to specify what, under contemporary conditions, would be a good society wherein one might lead a good life. The terms, of course, are derived from classical political science; the institutions to which they referred, however, do not exist. According to classical political science, two elements are involved: first, that it is large enough and affluent enough to enable those few who can lead a life of reason to be able to do so, and second, that the life of reason be a viable force in political life. That is, the essential constituent of a good society is the life of reason,[27] not constitutional form, not productivity, not technological cleverness. Beyond that, there are numerous options available to institutionalize the good society: one's guide in such matters, as Voegelin explained during the 1930s, is commonsense.

The following chapter examines From Enlightenment to Revolution, a text that was initially Part Eight of the History of Western Political Ideas. It constitutes both a last chapter in Voegelin's initial historiographic work and a splendid critical analysis of the major intellectual themes of modernity. Whatever the damage done to the common discourse of Western philosophy after Thomas and whatever the problems that arose in the wake of a growing intramundane sectarianism, the events and the interpretation of them as "progress" that we associate with the thinkers of the eighteenth century and after, constitute a radical break with the experiential continuity of the preceeding centuries.

NOTES

1 See below, Chapter Three.

2 Much of the unreferenced presentation is taken from Voegelin's manuscript. Until it is published, no purpose would be served by more explicit citation. The New Science, written after much of the manuscript was completed, may be read in part at least as an extended précis. In OH, II, 263ff, Voegelin discussed the topic of a popular dogmatic creed as the problem arose in Plato's Laws; in OH, II, 171ff, he discussed the related question of the "seemliness" of theological symbols. Other discussions of various aspects of the question may be found in: "The Oxford Political Philosophers;" "Necessary Moral Bases for Communication in a Pluralistic Society;" "Demokratie im neuen Europa;" "On Readiness to Rational Discussion;" "Industrial Society in Search of Reason;" "Verantwortung and Freiheit in Wirtschaft and Demokratie;" "Demokratie und Industriegesellschaft;" and "Liberalism and Its History." Full bibliographic information is given in the Appendix.

3 See below, Chapter Five.

4 "Political Theory and the Pattern of General History," 746-54.

5 Consider here Voegelin's remarks in "Configurations of History" and "Toynbee's History as a Search for Truth."

6 NSP, 52 ff. In Anam.-G, 283ff, 346ff and in OH, IV, Voegelin used the term "noetic interpretation" in an approximately identical sense. Both terms implied equally an avoidance of dogma and of historical relativism.

[7] These thorny methodological questions are explored in Voegelin's "Historiogenesis," the definitive version of which is in OH, IV, 59-113, and his article "Equivalences of Experience and Symbolization in History." These questions, along with the theory of consciousness that undergirds them are considered in a provisional way below in Chapters Five and Six.

[8] See OH, II, 274ff and III, 130f, 236ff.

[9] See, However, Voegelin's discussion in Anam., 37-60, and Chapter Six below.

[10] For a discussion of the original meaning and context of the image of the suffering servant, see OH, I, 488ff.

[11] OH, IV, 239ff. Voegelin's interpretations of Paul have occasioned considerable controversy. See the discussion by John Kirby "On Reading Eric Voegelin: A Note in the Critical Literature," in Kirby and William M. Thompson, eds., Voegelin and the Theologian: Ten Studies in Interpretation (New York and Toronto: Edwin Mellen, 1983), 24-60.

[12] Consider here Voegelin's remarks on the distinction between the pragmatic ecumene and the spiritual ecumene in OH, IV, 117ff; see also his comment on Polybius and Matthew in "World Empire and the Unity of Mankind," 184.

[13] See Voegelin's study of the Tamerlane myth, first published in 1937, "Das Timurbild der Humanisten: Eine Studie zur politischen Mythenbildung," in Anam.-G, 153-178. See also his studies, "The Mongol Orders of Submission to European Powers, 1245-1255," and "Machiavelli's Prince: Background and Formation."

[14] See below, Chapter Five.

[15] Cf. "Industrial Society in Search of Reason," 36.

[16] See Voegelin's detailed study, "Siger de Brabant."

[17] See Ernest Kantorowicz, _Frederick the Second, 1194-1250_ (New York: Smith, 1931), for details.

[18] See the references in "Siger de Brabant".

[19] For details, see _NSP_, chs. 4 and 6, and _ER_. See below, Chapter Three.

[20] These are the opening words to the Preface of _OH_, I.

[21] In addition to the detailed treatment in _NSP_, see also "Gnostische Politik;" _SPG_, _passim_; and "History and Gnosis."

[22] See "Industrial Society in Search of Reason," 36ff.

[23] See Voegelin's discussion of this topic in connection with Plato's _Laws_ in _OH_, III, 263ff.

[24] See Voegelin's analysis of Puritanism and its successors in _NSP_, 133ff.

[25] See Ellis Sandoz, "The Civil Theology of Liberal Democracy: Locke and his Predecessors," _Journal of Politics_ 34 (1972), 2-36.

[26] See "Industrial Society in Search of Reason," 37ff.

[27] For an elaboration of what the term "reason" meant within the context of classical experience, see Voegelin, "Reason: The Classic Experience," and the analysis in Chapter Six, below.

CHAPTER THREE

THE GENESIS OF MODERN UNREASON

I

Voegelin's earlier characterization of his own historical situation, as one who viewed the catastrophes of the century with a wake consciousness, describes as well the perennial situation of the philosopher. The contemporary context, for one as familiar with the textual interpretation and historical actions as Voegelin, had its genesis in the momentous upheavals of the eighteenth century. As John Hallowell remarked in his prefatory note to From Enlightenment to Revolution, "dream life usurping the place of wake life is the theme of this volume, when reason, torn loose from its moorings in the ground of being, seeks to create man-made constructions of reality in place of the mysterious reality of God's creation" (ER, ix). Thus through the ancient images of dream-life and wakefulness we have introduced: the misuse of reason in ideological language and the philosopher's self-conscious resistance to it, the human construction of second realities or possible realities and the topical problems these fabrications present to the critical intellect, the identification of the present epoch as one of crisis, and a summary identification of the source of that crisis. From Enlightenment to Revolution is a partial analysis of the spiritual going down of the West as it revealed itself during the eighteenth and nineteenth centuries in the writings of selected individuals. As analysis it is also a partial diagnosis; as partial diagnosis it is also, if not a partial cure then at least an innoculation. In Chapter Two we discussed the theme of civil theology in the History of Western Political Ideas. The disintegration of Christian and classical civil theologies or of antiquity as a spiritual reality in the psyche of European men was accelerated during the Enlightenment. Since then, as Leo Strauss used to say, we have been dwelling in a man-made cellar beneath Plato's cave.

*

In spite of the large number of texts and individuals subjected to analyses that will remain models of economy and critical clarity, we must stress the incompleteness of From Enlightenment to Revolution. By observing that no extended attention is given there to Montesquieu, Rousseau, the Scottish Enlightenment and its English aftermath, Schelling, Schopenhauer, or Nietzsche, one intends to blame neither author nor editor, but simply to express one's regret, and also one's hope that an additional selection from the History of Western Political Ideas will someday be made public.[1] A second preliminary observation concerns the circumstances surrounding the publication of this fragment some thirty years after it was written. Originally the entire study was commissioned by Fritz Morstein Marx as one of a series of short introductory texts to be published by McGraw Hill, but the manuscript grew far beyond the modest proportions originally envisaged. The Macmillan Company then agreed to publish the now multi-volume study and by 1950 or so several chapters had appeared in various forms.[2] But in the course of accumulating material Voegelin discovered that the conception of a history of ideas was methodologically untenable, and during the late 1940s he entered what he called a period of theoretical paralysis. Specifically, his study of Schelling's posthumous Philosophy of Mythology and Revelation and the Schellingian distinction between "negative philosophy," which dealt with concepts, ideas and, in general, the deductive and hypothetical, and "positive philosophy," which was concerned with the empirical, experiential dimensions of existence, brought to Voegelin's attention the limitations of the history of ideas as an organizing frame for political science. Rites and rituals, to say nothing of myths and revelations, simply were not "ideas".[3]

In 1951, Voegelin was asked to give a series of lectures at the University of Chicago. These appeared a year later under the title The New Science of Politics (and not under the original title, "Truth and Representation") and constitute sufficient evidence that Voegelin's "paralysis" had been overcome. Henceforth his work was centered around the terminology of "experience" and "symbolization." "Ideas," as Schelling had pointed out, were secondary inasmuch as they were derived from symbols or constitute transformations of symbols in such a way that the symbolic term no longer served as the expression of an experienced reality but rather took its meaning from an abstracted conceptual discourse or doctrine. The materials collected in the course of writing the History were to be integrated by way of this methodologically more adequate interpretative strategy in the projected six volumes of Order and History.

In the 1950s, a second[4] revision occurred. Several factors were involved. First of all, the empirical evidence upon which the theoretical insights were made was again growing beyond the point where the original number of volumes could contain all the material. More importantly, Voegelin found it no longer possible to accept as unproblematic the second major term of the original project, namely "history." That is, when one begins with something like Schelling's "positive philosophy," the empirical configurations of meaning, which are structured, as was noted, according to the pair of terms "experience" and "symbolization," do not necessarily arrange themselves along an historical time-line. As Voegelin remarked in the fourth volume of Order and History, analysis now had to move not simply backward and forward along a more or less visible historical course, it also had to move "sideways," "through a web of meaning with a plurality of nodal points".[5] History, then, understood as patterned events or meanings cannot itself constitute a "web of meaning" precisely because the "web" and its "nodal points" are identical to what is meant by "history." What we find analyzed in the most recent examples of Voegelin's work, to use an earlier formula, are "events in Being".[6] This analysis, as Voegelin's readers know, generates not only a specialized vocabulary that is, of itself, an extremely precise diagnostic instrument, but also one forged in such a way that the careful reader is enabled to recapture meditatively, and represent discursively, the original meaning intended. These brief comments on the direction of Voegelin's enterprise after his History of Western Political Ideas was abandoned may serve in a very provisional way to locate the fragment discussed in this chapter.

Let us return, however, to the 1940s, and see how the methodological problems, which later were so brilliantly resolved, appeared to Voegelin at that time. In 1944 Voegelin presented a "state of the discipline" report to the American Political Science Association on the topic of political theory.[7] Here he introduced a theme that reappeared not only in From Enlightenment to Revolution, but in his later work as well, namely, the problem of discerning empirical patterns in history.

The first general historical survey of political ideas, Voegelin began, was William A. Dunning's three-volume A History of Political Theories, first published in 1902. In this work Dunning followed a straight-line pattern that was derived from Christian theology of history, and could maintain its plausibility only so long as not too much was known by Westerners about non-Western events or so long these events could be interpreted as being peripheral to "real" or Western history. While ignorance and selective interpretation are far from ended, generally speaking, the work of Weber, Spengler and Toynbee has laid to rest the model of a Eurocentric single time-line as the sole standard of authentic history. Granting, then, the pattern of parallel historical streams or configurations, one still must determine its consequences for a history of political ideas. Now, Dunning was critical of Paul Janet, the

French historian, whose book his own was intended to replace, because Janet restricted the topic unduly and included only highly systematic arguments, mainly of an ethical nature. In contrast to "political science" in Janet's sense, Dunning wished to include any idea, whether scientific or not, that dealt with political authority in the context of the state. This allowed him to exclude the problem of authority in the family or in primitive tribes and also to include nonsystematic discussion of state authority.

The assumption concerning the admissibility of non-systematic ideas, Voegelin said, was a vast improvement over Janet, but the isolation of the political from the ethical, theological, and legal contexts of society was to produce curious results. Far Eastern theory was eliminated as a matter of course. In fact, this did little damage to the concept of Western political thought as the historical links between the two were tenuous. Less acceptable was his elimination of the ancient Near East and the European Middle Ages on the grounds that they mixed up mythical or theological ideas with political ones. The basis for this elimination lay in Dunning's notion of progress, by which he meant the separation of politics from theology, ethics and metaphysics and its development as an autonomous sphere of meaning. By this largely unexamined device, there were two periods of progress in "political theory," one in classical antiquity and one at the close of the medieval period, extending into the present. But, Voegelin remarked, one cannot justify "by any standards of scientific method" the "elimination as irrelevant of a phase of history which is in direct continuity with our own, because its structure of political ideas differs from ours." Instead, the historian "has to follow with impartial loyalty the structure of theory as it reveals itself in history, whether it reflects the problems of a differentiated sphere of politics, or whether it reflects an undifferentiated complex of community order including 'morals, economics, government, religion, and law.'"

In principle, George Sabine's A History of Political Theory (1939, 4th ed. 1973), with its division of the historical material into the theory of the city-state, of the universal community, and of the national state, met this methodological objection. Other ways of organizing the historical material may be more satisfactory than Sabine's (and Voegelin found the pattern proposed by Toynbee and the Cambridge Ancient and Cambridge Medieval Histories to be superior), but these are more refinements than methodological alternatives.[8] Thus, in this short article of 1944 we find a concise elaboration of the principle that eventually led Voegelin to abandon the framework of his History of Western Political Ideas; this principle also accounts for the seventeen-year gap between the third and fourth volumes of Order and History, namely fidelity to the empirical patterns that are revealed historically.

We have as yet spoken rather loosely about "ideas" and would make more precise what Voegelin intended by the term during this period. In one of the earliest articles Voegelin published after emigrating to the United States, he provided English-speaking readers with a dis-

tillation of the arguments of the two books he had written
earlier on the problem of race as a political symbol.[9]
The first section of this paper was entitled "The Problem
of the Political Idea" and is the most systematic available
statement of Voegelin's contemporary meaning.

The race idea, Voegelin began, is to be distinguished
from the concept of race as the term is used in natural
science, eugenics, and studies of social relations between
Americans whose forebears came from Europe or Asia with
those who were brought from Africa. "When we speak of
the race idea we have in mind chiefly the idea as it is
used by modern creeds, of the type of National Socialism,
in order to integrate a community spiritually and politically." An "idea" in this first sense, then, is part
of the intellectual baggage that constitutes what contemporary sociologists call a "belief-system." It is most
emphatically not a body of knowledge that may be true
or false, "but a political idea in the technical sense
of the word. A political idea does not attempt to describe
social reality as it is, but it sets up symbols, be
they single language units or more elaborate dogmas,
which have the function of creating the image of a group
as a unit." Consequently, criticism of the race idea
or the idea of revolution because they do not constitute
empirically verifiable propositions is beside the point
"because it is not the function of an idea to describe
social reality, but to assist in its constitution."
Not that ideas are necessarily pure fantasies but that,
by and large, they are based on an element of empirical
reality that then may be transfigured intellectually
into a public symbol. The public symbol, the political

idea in the technical sense, "uses the datum of empirical
reality in order to represent by means of that single,
comparatively simple element a diffuse field of reality
as a unit." Such representation is what endows this
unit with meaning as a race, class, nation, etc.

Distinct from the term "political idea" is what
Voegelin called an "idea of man." By this term Voegelin
indicated a realm of discourse covered by Max Scheler's
"philosophical anthropology".[10] In a review of a book
by Huntington Cairns,[11] for example, Voegelin criticized
the author for his inability to develop criteria of
relevance for selecting facts and events as having some
bearing upon the topics examined by the social sciences.
Cairns was silent about this crucial matter "for the
good reason" that he "has no overt philosophy of man
and of his place in society and the world at large that
could tell him what is relevant in the world of man and
society; the whole branch of knowledge that goes today
under the name of philosophical anthropology is
nonexistent for the author. Unless we have an idea of
man, we have no frame of reference for the designation
of human phenomena as relevant or irrelevant." Clearly
then, an idea of man can be in conflict with a political
idea, inasmuch as the former attempts to describe human
existence in a broader context than the reality of a
political or social unit. And, indeed, there are conflicts
among ideas of man, which is to say there are disagreements
about the principles of philosophical anthropology.[12]

What then? Are we able to choose between more and
less adequate principles? If so, how? Or, are we at

the mercy of anybody's opinion about the nature of man? How, in short, to deal with the false prophet? Voegelin had two answers. Neither of these today would have seemed to him complete, because both were based essentially upon common sense and upon historical contingencies. In the first place, he said, there is the weight of social institutions that serves as a damper on bizarre fancies, insofar as the idea of man expressed in institutions influences the amplitude of effective disagreement. Secondly, such errors as exist within this establishment are open to correction insofar as they serve as topics for analysis and discussion. Accordingly, beneath the disagreements among philosophers "there is a convergence towards standards, which makes it impossible to claim the successful construction of a system unless the anthropology underlying it gives due weight to the various elements of human nature." This is not to say, however, that one should expect a steady improvement in the social sciences "for the idea of man is not a datum of the external world, but a creation of the human spirit, undergoing historical changes, and it has to be recreated by every generation and by every single person." Deficiencies and inadequacies of scientific discourse thus result not simply from ignorance but (perhaps more often) from idiosyncracies to be found in the fundamental attitudes of scholars with respect to their idea of man.[13]

Again, one may ask: what then? And again Voegelin provided two answers, one that described the actual historical contingencies for maintaining a more or less comprehensive idea of man, and another that carried out <u>in</u> <u>concreto</u> a "correction."

The dampening effect of institutions upon the outbreak of revolutionary ideas as effective political forces is in large measure related to the legitimacy they have obtained through generations of development. In France and England, for example, the creation of state institutions may be traced back to medieval monarchy so that, with the advent of new sectors of the population to political visibility, these eruptions could more or less easily be integrated into existing structures. So much is obvious to every first-year student of comparative politics. What is often forgotten, however, is that the creation of the national state is not simply a question of creating or taking over an already existing bureaucratic apparatus. All the national states were at one time new, and the period during which they came of age decisively influenced the political ideas that informed the attitudes of the newly visible strata. It was important, for example, that the English Revolution was understood by those who went through it, from the top to the bottom of the social and political hierarchy and on both sides, in Christian metaphors and symbols. In later centuries, this meant that political reformers would be more mindful of their religious predecessors, would feel the weight of "tradition," and would be unlikely to accept uncritically ideas that were grossly at variance with it. Likewise in France, the 19th century diffusion of ideas, such as the rights of man and the liberties of the citizen, within a stable monarchic structure meant that, on the whole, the French have resisted the ideas accompanying the revolutionary movements of this century.

The great contrast here is made by Italy, Germany, the Soviet Union, and a host of "new nations." In Voegelin's words: "Roughly speaking, and omitting some qualifications, one might say that in a revolutionary situation, when there is no resistance through the authority of established symbols, the current type of social symbols will prevail".[14] Accordingly, those revolutions that occurred earliest will preserve more of the symbolism and corresponding sentiments and beliefs of prior Christian and classical sensibility. It has often been observed, for example, that the Wesleyan societies and Methodist churches served to restrain the industrial and urban poor of Britain from wholeheartedly embracing the radical revolutionary ideas of continental ideological movements. This historical contingency is not, however, a "heritage" upon which the heirs of the English Revolution around the world may complacently sit, which brings us to Voegelin's second point.

The French have a saying, that the English are afraid of philosophy because it poses a threat to their cherished common sense. An English philosopher would reply that Sartre's Being and Nothingness is a misuse of the copula. One sympathizes with the Englishman trying to make common sense from Sartre's book, but one sees as well the point of the acerbic continental. Speaking very broadly, one may say that precisely because of the stability of their political institutions, the states that fell heir to the English revolution have grown insensitive to the fundamental problems of political existence. Where national institutions do not enjoy the authority of age, where the society is disrupted by military defeat, economic turmoil, or civil war, and where sectarian movements have replaced the national community as the society that is organized for political action, "there a science of principles will develop, and especially of philosophical anthropology, to the neglect of an analysis of institutions --though the philosopher will be at a loss what to do with his knowledge in an environment that seethes with ideological enthusiasm, has no use for reason, and hates the dianoetic excellences".[15] In spite of the very uneven quality of continental European speculations, it is surely uncontentious to say that French and German (or German exile) scholars have provided the most intellectually stimulating work of the past two generations. If we attend to the political and social context from which those scholars emerged, it does not take a great deal of imagination to see why. A similar argument might be made with respect to Solzhenitsyn.

Here the contrast with Britain, the United States, and the former settlement colonies such as Canada and New Zealand is most obvious. In Voegelin's words: "There the analysis will start from the treasure of institutions, working its way cautiously toward principles in order not to lose anything of the truth that has accumulated in an organization functioning so well for so long --even at the risk of leaving principles in a penumbra where they remain indistinguishable from the state of England." Principles of government have likewise been difficult to distinguish from the constitutional tradition of the United States (as with Senator Ervin during the Senate hearings on the Watergate affair) or of Canada (as with the Parliamentary debates over the proclamation of the War Measures Act in 1970), or of Australia (as with the conflict between Prime Minister Whitlam and the Governor General, Sir John Kerr). In these countries and others that may enjoy a long period of relative stability, the danger is that prudential constitutional devices, which were designed to meet specific conditions and to preserve a particular political order, will be mistaken for fundamental principles of universal or quasi-universal validity.

In other words, "the cult of political institutions as incarnations of principles depends on the suspension of theoretical animation".[16] Instead of theoretical discussion, one engages in an elaborate analysis of the constituent elements of the reigning civil theology and a cautious elaboration of how to adapt it to new problems. If we restrain analysis to the beliefs of citizens that sustain a state, we write the history of ideas, dogmas, and beliefs (or perhaps give it a systematic exposition), but only by assuming these opinions are in fact a critical theory of man, a philosophical anthropology properly speaking, can the analysis be called a political philosophy. And, of course, by making the assumption and acting on it in composing one's analyses, one has no way of telling if it was valid. This eclipse of political philosophy by civil theology is a matter of some moment, for in the absence of a science of principles, one is helpless before the sheer stream of events. The work of civil theologians is hardly worthless, even for the philosophically inclined historian, but it is also true that they avoid "the decisive issue in a philosophy of politics," namely whether a given political order "offers the opportunity for full actualization of human nature. The fully actualized man is the spoudaios, the mature man, who had developed his dianoetic excellences and whose life is oriented by his noetic self." If this issue is avoided, the so-called political philosophies that result will be no more than "a parlour game in which one can indulge as long as the surrounding society contains enough Christian substance to make at least the worst sort of good consciences socially ineffective; but even under such favorable conditions (as they still exist in England) this nihilistic theory of conscience contributes to the intellectual and moral confusion which paves the way for the best of all consciences, viz., that of the totalitarian killers".[17]

Let us draw together some of the threads of the analysis so far. The "idea" of race or of revolution or, in general, political ideas, constitutes an essential element of political reality because they serve as the means whereby social or political units understand themselves as meaningful groups, whether the group be an aristocracy of blood, a master-race, a chosen people, a revolutionary vanguard. Political ideas, therefore, serve as topics for analysis within the discipline of political science. Analysis, in turn, presupposes a philosophical anthropology, an "idea" of man, which establishes criteria of truth and error, right and wrong, justice and injustice. In general, an "idea" of man establishes criteria of relevance with regard to "a truthful account of the structure of reality" (NSP, 5). Thus, it serves to constitute the essential element of a theoretical attitude towards the world, and hence also serves as the great diagnostic instrument of social and political disorder.

A second major point concerned the unevenness of political ideas as judged by the criteria of philosophical anthropology. Some political orders, those of Western Europe and the former settlement colonies of Britain, have preserved in their political institutions and in the beliefs that inform them, more of the medieval Christian and classical pagan idea of man than have those of Eastern Europe. Parts of the world that have had European ideas thrust upon them along with the destructiveness of imperial power have had very little exposure to the full idea of man in the Western sense, though here too there are significant differences.[18] But even in Western Europe and in political orders emergent from various British empires, which happen to be favored by historical contingencies, there is a constant danger that, regarding this institutional heritage with justifiable pride, its parochial features and its civil theology will be mistaken for principles of philosophical politics and a comprehensive anthropology. In Platonic terms, this would be to confuse orthe doxa with episteme. Consequently, the political philosopher must analyze the more noble and true political ideas as well as foul and false ones.

It may well turn out that the most comprehensive and incisive formulations of philosophical anthropology

are created by persons living in polities whose actual
political order is in sharpest contrast with the Western
civilizational heritage. This is one factor that
explains, for example, the great difference between
Anglo-American and continental European philosophizing.
One may reiterate as well that it is one factor explaining
Voegelin's wakefulness. However that may be, the principle may be taken as established that it is political
science based upon a comprehensive philosophical anthropology, and not upon an orthodox civil theology or the
contingencies of ancient and noble political institutions
that the critical justification of political order eventually rests. Or, as Voegelin put it in From Enlightenment
to Revolution: "The historian of ideas has to do more
than to report the doctrines advanced by a thinker or
to give an account of a few great systems. He has to
explore the growth of sentiments, which crystallize into
ideas, and he has to show the connection between ideas
and the matrix of sentiments in which they are rooted.
The idea has to be studied, not as a concept, but as a
symbol which draws its life from sentiments; the idea
grows and dies with the sentiments which engender its
formulation" (ER, 68). Let us turn directly, then, to
Voegelin's application of these philosophical and
methodological postulates.

*

It would be a gross impertinence to presume to
condense the argument of one whose powers of concise
presentation so far exceed one's own. One can scarcely
but hint at the extraordinary precision of analysis and

the splendid powers of synthesis that order a vast amount
of factual detail into what is probably the most accessible
of Voegelin's books in English. What I shall do is
focus upon the two themes already introduced in abstracto,
as it were: the question of meaning and historical
patterns, and the question of philosophical anthropology
as a diagnostic instrument.

In the two hundred and fifty years or so prior to
the publication of Voltaire's Essai sur les Moeurs et
l'Esprit des Nations, around 1750, several historical
events conspired to create in the minds of those who
reflected upon them a sense that an epoch had ended:
the Church no longer existed as an institutional representation of mankind; a plurality of sovereign states in a
quasi-constitutional balance with one another extended
as ultimate political units with little or no relation
to the Empire; the new world had been discovered and
was in the process of being settled by Europeans; trade
and intercourse with Asiatic civilization was begun more
or less on a basis of equality; and finally, a non-Christian
idea of man was expounded as the basis for law, politics,
and ethics. That something new was in the air was obvious
to any who had the leisure to consider the question.
One such, the Marquise du Chatelet-Lorraine, expressed
the new self-understanding in two queries, written in
the margin of Bossuet's Discours sur l'Histoire
Universelle (1681). In the first, she questioned the
significance of the Jews for "history" and in the second,
she wondered about the preeminence of Rome, as compared
to the much greater significance that ought be accorded
the Russian Empire (ER, 4-5).

The Marquise did not, of course, initiate a historiographic revolution. Rather, her intelligent näiveté served as evidence that one had already taken place at a much deeper level. Since Bossuet's Romanocentric bias was a consequence of his Christianity, the Marquise was in fact raising a challenge to "the Christian idea of universality" on the basis of an empirical knowledge of human history that appeared to go beyond the bounds of Christian terminology. That is, Christianity was an event in "history," which in turn was meaningful on the basis of some other idea; it was no longer understood as the spiritual drama of humanity whose successive scenes constitute the pragmata of history. There was no longer a difference between sacred history and profane history, a symbolism whose roots went back millennia, but only a single secular history, an inner-worldly chain of events, an immanent stream of genesis. As a consequence, sheer quantitative greatness became the defining factor of significance: Rome had no universalist symbolical meaning and was retired to the status of a limited historical phenomenon.

Voltaire was impressed with the remarks of his hostess and patron and undertook to respond to them in his Essai, which he described as a "philosophy of history," and understood the term to be in direct opposition to Bossuet's "theology" of history. Voltaire conceived his enterprise as a supplement and correction to Bossuet's Discours, but, as was Bossuet, so Voltaire was faced with the problem of organizing his materials. The tacit interpretative principle he used was that an empirically complete account would yield up a universal meaning, which in turn presupposed that history as a whole was, in principle, knowable, if not known. In Christianity this difficulty is met (if one may be permitted the use of such language) by anticipation of the Parousia. But when the experience of anticipation is lost and the second coming turned into a hypostatized future event, Christianity becomes a parochial civilization prejudice because, for example, the Chinese have never heard about it. Clearly somehow the Chinese must be taken into account, but just as clearly the way to do so is not by trying to write an historical encyclopedia. Since one cannot know the meaning of history unless it has been completed, unless the occurrence of subsequent pragmata constitute nothing new, and since as an interpretation, Voltaire's "philosophy of history" must order events in some way or other if they are to form a coherent story, necessarily he had to introduce certain additional principles in order to replace the now defunct Christian ones.

For Voltaire the two most important were the general idea of an evolution of opinion and the specification of its direction, from the "barbarian rusticity" of earlier days to the "_politesse_" of Voltaire's. When people stopped believing emperors and popes, mankind was on its way towards truth and reason. How did we know this? Because Voltaire was pointing it out in his _Essai_. Then how did Voltaire know? "On this point the argument is somewhat hazy, as occurs so frequently with Voltaire when a serious question had to be answered" (_ER_, 10). While not a model of close reasoning, Voltaire's argument did introduce the chief category for inventing secular history, a category, moreover, for which an equivalent is to

be found in all of Voltaire's successors: the human
spirit and its changes. In short, "the historian selects
a partial structure of meaning, declares it to be total,
and arranges the rest of the historical materials more
or less elegantly around this center of meaning" (ER,
11). The structure so selected is given whatever importance it has because it serves as the vehicle for expressing
the contemporary sense of epoch and the intramundane
sentiments that are its most apparent spiritual feature.
But because in fact sentiments change, the choice of
structure to give meaning to history also changes. This
is hardly surprising, for we are adrift on a sea of
random potentiality. In Platonic terms, it is an imaginary
world of genesis without the firmness of ousia.

The origin of this instability of religious sentiment
lies in the charms of variations, in a preference for
novelty over truth, for poetry over philosophy. In
Bossuet's idiom of ecclesiastical politics, the origin
of instability may be found in the successful challenge
to the authority of tradition: once broken by an individual innovator, subsequent innovations are defined by nothing more than the personal style of the individual. In
particular, for Bossuet, the conflict between the meaning
of Christian history and the literally idiotic meanings
of other historical models amounted to a conflict between
the Church and several heresies. Since change appears
to be as permanent as a desire for permanence, one may
generalize the question as concerning the creation of a
spiritual substance that is stable (if not permanent)
under conditions of intellectual ferment, and the
accompanying creation and dissolution of communities.

Bossuet's arguments of 1678, as Hooker's analysis of the Puritan soul two generations earlier, may well be beyond dispute, but more is involved in the civilizational dynamics of modernity than the traditional principles of Christian theology of history. Overlooking the series of famous and historic political and intellectual failures on the part of the Church, Voegelin described "somewhat drastically" the deepest sentiment causing the spiritual disturbances of the West since the Middle Ages as follows: "the bearers of Western civilization do not want to be a senseless appendix to the history of antiquity; they want to understand their civilizational existence as meaningful." Consequently, if the Church is unable to interpret the presence of God in their history, people will scurry after strange gods that at least take an interest in their doings, however unsatisfactory they may be in other respects. The crucial issue, in Voegelin's words, is "that man in search of authority cannot find it in the Church, through no fault of his own" (ER, 22-23). Or, in terms of the problem of historical meaning, if Bossuet's formulation of historia sacra leaves no room for Chinese civilization, is it really a great surprise to hear that Voltaire placed an icon of Confucius above his bedstead (Sancte Confuci, ora pro nobis) and evoked a new "sacred history" that would take the great oriental civilizations into account?

This issue is further clarified with Voegelin's discussion of Turgot.[19] In 1750, at age 23, Turgot gave two lectures at the Sorbonne that developed a clear and austere doctrine of progress. The question he asked himself was: how comes it that mathematics was more advanced than physics, which in turn was more advanced (in the sense of providing more certain knowledge) than other ways of interpreting the external world. Turgot formulated his answer on the basis of the simplified Lockean epistemology, then current in France: all knowledge and all ideas were derived from sensation; mathematics dealt with ideas only, whereas physics operated with the external world as well, which meant that the purity of ideas was lost, errors were frequent, corrections were slow. In particular, we tend to project into external worldly being a structure and a process analogous to human being. Thus, we think all that occurred externally that was not of human agency was caused by gods, who were imagined to be analogous to humans. Gradually these anthropomorphic prejudices were purged (and Turgot explained at some length the details of the process) and were replaced by abstract expressions, which referred to nothing real but were simply less fantastic anthropomorphic divinities, which in turn gave way to proper observation of the mechanical interaction of bodies that lent itself to mathematical expression and experimental (or "experiential" --the word is the same in French) verification (ER, 88-89). The process of purification was called by Turgot, "progress."

This precise definition of progress enabled one to circumscribe a basic empirical core of meaning, the development of mathematics and physics, as distinct from an evocative meaning that was obtained or was made the criterion for meaning as such. The misuse of the basic meaning was not absent from Turgot, and Voegelin provided a scrupulous analysis of several instances and implications (ER, 91-109. Yet in spite of Turgot's mutilation of Christian sacred history, he did introduce some genuinely empirical questions with respect to profane history, concerning the units of analysis, the flux and reflux of power within the units, and so on. In addition, he retained the commonsense observation that human beings show different degrees of spiritual strength that are irreducible to other factors, including "civilizational progress." Thus, for Turgot, "however much civilization progresses, man does not progress. The social environment may change in such a manner that it favors the unfolding and effectiveness of talents but the talents do not change" (ER, 108). Accordingly, while there can be progress in the arts, science, technology, economics, politics, morals, and sheer knowledge, the question of man remains the same, whether in primitive or polite civilization. Indeed, Voegelin remarked, the differentiation of "social progress" may be so great and the society that results may be so complicated that the available "talents" may be insufficient to continue the momentum or even maintain it at a given level.

Turgot's analysis proceeded far enough to distinguish the course of civilizational dynamics, of which the development of mathematics and physics is the resplendent paradigm, from the constant and central political problem of the existence of man in society, which he expressed in terms of the irreducible distribution of talent. The difficulty in integrating the two problems is suggested by the following question: when the civilizational dynamics have destroyed the existing social structures by which "talents" are recruited to govern, what is to replace them? (That <u>something</u> must replace traditional structures of recruitment is apparent from the constancy of the problem of the distribution of talent.) This question received theoretical attention later with the elite studies of Mosca, Pareto, and Dorso, and was analyzed by Toynbee under the category of "creative minority." It received immediate practical attention with Turgot's progressivist successors and was called by Voegelin "the short circuit evocation of elites," by which he meant a "readiness to embark on the task of forming a new elite without properly gauging its magnitude" (<u>ER</u>, 111-112).

The historical pattern thrown up by the "age of enlightenment" or the "age of revolution" by way of the several progressivist thinkers exhibits, therefore, the following complexities: on the one hand there was a widespread consciousness of epoch on the part of educated as well as uneducated members of society. Along with this vast civilizational change, the incompetence of traditional elites to deal with it was becoming more evident; in Toynbee's terminology, the creative minority had become a dominant minority. This shift in social order brought into view the theoretical insight that the problem of political order was a general one, separable from the contingencies of the particular upheaval that occasioned it. At the same time, practical steps were taken to replace the discredited dominant minority with a new creative minority, but, as this action was undertaken in order to circumvent the previous theoretical insight, it is entirely accurate to apply the adjective "short-circuit" to the measures proposed. All that would occur would be the replacement of one dominant minority with another.

In this new historical configuration, two immediate courses appeared open. Either one could drop the emphasis on progress and concentrate on the problems of social disintegration,(the reality of which was unfolding behind the progressive rhetoric),or one could attempt to deal with the autonomous problem of political order and yet not give up the benefits of progress by adopting one or another of the "short-circuit" programmes. Yet there was a third, more difficult option as well at which Voegelin did no more than hint. The problem turns on the very practical question introduced earlier concerning modern men in search of authority and unable to find it in traditional organizations such as the Church. Obviously, one cannot throw in one's lot with the progressive, and the patient theoretical analysis of the complex does not necessarily result in persuasion. One may, however, describe the practical measures required even though one is unable to supply them oneself. Part of the answer, Voegelin said "would have to be a new Christian philosophy of history and of mythical symbols that would make intelligible, firstly, the new dimension of meaning which has accrued to the historical existence of Christianity through the fact that the Church has survived two civilizations; and it would make intelligible, secondly, the myth as an objective language for the expression of a transcendental irruption, more adequate and exact as an instrument of expression than any rational system of symbols, not to be misunderstood in a literalism, which results from opacity, nor reduced to an experiential

level of psychology" (ER, 22). This was the task Voegelin
said required a new Thomas, not a neo-Thomist. The
task of the political philosopher, however, is more modest.

If it is a misuse of Turgot's "thread of progress"
to puff it up from a relatively narrow statement concerning
the growth of mathematics and physics to a general statement of historical meaning, let us then consider its
basic sense. According to Turgot, the movement from
anthropomorphic projections to scientific accounts of
the interrelation of physical effects expressed the
fullest and most comprehensive development of the human
intellect. When, however, one attempts to trace the
development of the intellect from one stage to another
one finds no identity of function or significance but
rather a distinction of levels of meaning. A hurricane,
for example, is both a manifestation of Min, or Zeus,
or Thor, or Parjanya, and a mathematical model for a
cloud physicist. There is no progress in understanding
as one moves from "primitive" or "anthropomorphic" rituals
to the sophistication of the Navier-Stokes equations,
both of which may deal with "hurricanes".[20] Rather,
there is "the transition from speculation on substance
to the science of phenomena. In the anthropomorphic
phase the knowledge of phenomena is still embedded in
the knowledge of substances; in the positive phase the
knowledge of phenomena is differentiated into the critical
system of mathematized science. This development in
itself certainly is an advance of our knowledge of
phenomena, but it is not a progress of the human intellect."
To the extent that knowledge of phenomena is held to
exhaust one's understanding of the world and so to eclipse

knowledge of substance, "the transition is distinctly a retrogression." An analysis of the concept of progress simply brings to light the separation of phenomena from substance, which is to say it dissolves the two components that progressive rhetoric attempts to unite.

Having analyzed progress as a topic, which is the initial task of the political scientist, the question of understanding the now disjunctive component parts theoretically then arises. There is no problem with the sciences of phenomena: on the one hand, there exists the concrete practice of natural science and technology and, on the other, there exists the history of this science and technology. But what of speculation upon substance, the essential question in any philosophy of man in society? The progressives, to repeat, excluded the topic from the final phase of development. If, however, "we do not exclude it, but conscientiously continue the line of thought initiated in the description of the first phase, the question will arise: what becomes of the problem of substance once it has passed beyond the stage of anthropomorphic symbolism?" Here Voegelin referred us to Schelling's answer, "his philosophy of the theogonic process" and "the new roles assigned to the protodialectic experiences and their dialectical elaboration." But, he added, we also know that Schelling found this answer unsatisfactory because philosophical speculation is "a poor substitute for the forceful imagery of mythology." Consequently, we are brought once again to the question of a new myth, because, "when it comes to the symbolization of substances, the myth is a more adequate mode of expression than a critical concept, which can only clarify our experience but cannot incarnate the substance itself." The charm of poetry consists in the immediacy of its experience; accordingly, the disintegration of a myth implies the disintegration "of the sacramental bond between men who hold it in common." Brought again to the same question, we are likewise faced with the same two options, the contemplative and the activist.

The activist response, which threw out speculation on substance as being inappropriate for the last phase of history, reintroduced an equivalent speculation in the form of new religious cults and movements. These several new spiritual foundations, from the bizarre Saint-Simonians encamped at Suez awaiting the advent of the Great Mother to the recent cult of Che Guevera, are incidental accompaniments to the problem of evoking new elites. "This question of the spiritual 'short-circuit' forms part of the general problem of the pneumopathology of the crisis" (ER, 117).

The contemporary contemplative response was found in Schelling's Philosophy of Mythology and Revelation, a work, the importance of which, for Voegelin's own philosophy of mythology and revelation, we have already indicated. For Schelling, "the spiritual process in which the symbols of myth and dogma are created is recovered from the unconscious through anamnesis (recollection), and the symbols actually created in the course of human history are interpreted as meaningful phases of the theogonic process, manifesting itself in history on rising levels of spiritual consciousness." In this theoretical attitude myth is grasped reflectively as expressing a spiritual reality for which later expressions are simply more differentiated equivalents rather than supercessions that render myth invalid. Through an intentional act one can, to use Polanyi's term, "in-dwell" a myth and experience imaginatively the meaning it expresses; one can explore equivalent myths and articulate discursively a second-order conceptual summary in a theoretical mode.[21] This was the principle of Schelling's interpretation of pagan myths, Oriental imagery, Roman Catholicism, and Protestantism, of Bergson's Two Sources of Morality and Religion, and has, through Bergson, influenced Toynbee as well. Furthermore, as is evident, Voegelin's own theory of history was decisively influenced by these thinkers.

To conclude this first topic, namely the problem of historical patterns and meaning, let us consider briefly Voegelin's analysis of the structural dilemma of progressivist historiography. We have seen with the Marquise du Chatelet, Voltaire, and their successors, that the great opponent was Christianity. When the vast dramatic sweep from Creation to the Last Judgment is simply expelled, one must necessarily begin anew from the existing critical situation, with the past behind and the future ahead, and neither the one nor the other present.[22] Now, the present, actual, historic situation is a matter of contingent fact that might have been otherwise (hence, the famous problem of Cleopatra's nose). Accordingly, it has to be shored up with supporting doctrine that imparts to those who believe on it a feeling that this particular present is of greater worth than any other.

In order to make the present contingent actuality "authoritative" for all other presents, it must be protected against both the past and the future. It is easy enough to guard against the authority of the past: it is simply declared to be obsolete and no longer to be taught. More aggressively, old books are expurgated or pulped and history (sometimes very recent history) is rewritten so as to conform to the authoritative standards of the present. This practice, common among contemporary statesmen who take seriously Voltaire's quip, that history is a pack of tricks we play on the dead, needs hardly be enlarged upon.

Protection against the future is rather more subtle, because the idea of stopping any further progress seems to contradict the idea of progress itself. Nevertheless, insofar as the progressive conceives the future as a continuation, or even as the perfection, of the present, he necessarily conceives it as a projection of the present, which is to say, "the idea of progress is static" (ER, 84).[23] Unfortunately for progressive thinkers the world is not static and history cannot be "stopped" simply upon hearing the progressive word. The result is a succession of "new worlds that will be old tomorrow, at the expense of old worlds that were new yesterday".[24] The documents that project these new/old worlds are informed by a mood of anxiety that is poorly covered over by the jargon of dialectics and hyperdialectics. The mood arises in the first place because of a fear that the future will not conform to the intellectual projection of the individual, in which case the entire enterprise would be senseless, an admission no progressive could possibly make. In short, the idea of progress, born from a consciousness of crisis and a very real experience of discontinuity, has built into its own doctrine, which attempts to obliterate both past and future, a structural guarantee that the discontinuity will persist and the spiritual crisis for which progressivism is a symptom rather than a solution, will continue.

Of course, one is not obliged to become a progressivist intellectual as the example of Schelling and his successors so clearly shows. The price of resistance is that a "philosophy of the spirit in history and politics" will run into conflict with the new and publicly effective religious orthodoxies (ER, 117). The pragmatic results will vary according to the nature and intensity of belief with which the new creeds are held. Theoretically, however, "the spiritualist is faced implacably by the united front of liberal progressives, Fascists, Communists and National Socialists" (ER, 118). This otherwise quarrelsome lot are agreed at least in their opposition to the restoration of the sources of spirituality to public prominence. We are brought, therefore, to our second major topic, the question of an image of man.

We may begin by considering Voltaire's attack on Christianity. The truth of Christianity is to be found in the spiritual process of the soul tending towards the cognition, by faith, of realities the experience of which is not given to faculties whose objects of cognition are existent phenomena. In the absence of this process, the dogmatic formulae are turned into "positions" to which one may or may not choose to subscribe, or choose to force others to accept. Considering the contemporary wars of religion, it is perhaps not surprising that one whose powers of spiritual insight were as Voltaire's would reject the (to him) incomprehensible spiritual process along with an entirely comprehensible dogma. The byword of contemporary computer programmers, "garbage in, garbage out," applies equally to enlightened criticism of Christianity: the garbage in was Voltaire's dogmatic criticism of dogma; the garbage out was his own enlightened counter-dogma.

In place of God who is experienced as the source of grace is the God who is a likely hypothesis, since the world described by Newton's laws appeared to demand a superior artificer. Or, even if not a likely hypothesis (Laplace found he could do without it soon enough) then at least God was useful as, in Voltaire's words, the man who "reasons" was perverse and the fear of divine punishment was needed to keep him in line. The soul as the sensorium of transcendence was replaced with "thought" and, replacing the ethical norm of a spiritually integrated person, was the person who was useful to the human species because he was moved by compassion. This sentiment inspiring useful deeds implied that one who was not useful did not count ethically or, as Hannah Arendt said in her analysis of the problem, such a person was "superfluous." Behind these familiar and high-sounding phrases "looms the virtuous terreur of Robespierre and the massacres of the later humanitarians whose hearts are filled with compassion to the point that they are willing to slaughter one-half of mankind in order to make the other half happy" (ER, 28). In contrast to a compassionate and useful humanity (which, as Scheler has argued, was a product of resentment anyhow) is "the healthy Christian cynicism which is aware of the precarious ascendancy of the spirit over the passions and takes its precautions" (ER, 28-29).

Not only was Christianity mutilated by enlightenment, so too was philosophy. Worse, the chief term used to express the mutilation was "reason." It is true that Voltaire directed his attacks against religious wars and persecution, that is, against ecclesiastical intellectuals "who bring human sacrifices to dogmatic subtleties which should be of secondary importance as compared with the substance of faith" (ER, 34), and that he would have been equally angry with war and persecution in the name of progress, the proletariat, the nation, or the race, it is still true to point out that he grossly misconstrued the residual sense of the term "reason." In place of the immediate spiritual experience is the aforementioned mediation of Newtonian science. This intellectual structure is animated by the fundamental sentiment of an "intrawordly faith in a society which finds coherence through compassion and humanity," where humanity is "a general disposition in man arising out of his biological structure" (ER, 29). Voltaire did not systematize the new sentiments into formulae for action but remained in a state of "prerevolutionary suspense." He had abandoned the old spirituality and he fought for the establishment of the new, but he did not attempt to bring it about himself. His was "a realm not of the spirit, but between the spirits, where man can live for a moment in the illusion that he can, by discarding the old spirit, free himself of the evil which invariably arises from the life of the spirit in the world, and that the new world will create a world without evil" (ER, 32-33).

With Helvetius, Voltaire's younger contemporary, there is a shift in sentiment away from compassion and towards engineering. Helvetius was searching for a new basis of morality and, since for him as well, immediate spiritual experience did not exist, he looked to the immediacy of bodily experience, which he believed conformed to mechanical laws. Here we find systematized in the category of genealogy, the already existing, if somewhat inchoate, doctrine of explaining the higher by the lower, the noble by the base, the psychic by the somatic, the spiritual by the biological, and so forth. Accordingly, one could describe one's bodily passions and manipulate them in order to achieve the desired result. The significance of this complex of sensualism, hedonism, and utilitarianism, whose contemporary avatars range from government by an elite skilled in managing a population through public relations, to Gestalt-therapy among the Redwoods, to yoga on television, comes not from its adequacy as a philosophical anthropology (since vast blocks of human experience are ignored) but from its being a confession of faith in a dogma of wordly social salvation. In this connection, Helvetius was the first to see that if the insight into spiritual realities was lost, "a philosophy of social justice has to rely on the historical evolution of economic institutions as its basis" (ER, 62). Later variations of a Benthamite and Marxist type simply chose different categories of society to be the chief beneficiaries of the essentially egalitarian (because we are all equal biological organisms) justice of animal laborans.

The skeletal outline of Voegelin's analysis presented here should suffice in a negative way to suggest the inadequacies of the new image of man. There was, in short, "a reduction of man to the level of utilitarian existence...through the atrophy of the intellectual and spiritual substance of man. In the progressive, positivist movement since the middle of the eighteenth century, as well as with the followers of the movement, the term man no longer designates the mature man of the humanist and Christian tradition, but only the crippled, utilitarian fragment" (ER, 95). Not only was the image of the individual person eclipsed, of necessity the image of mankind was also replaced. The Christian image of mankind is "of a community whose substance consists of the spirit in which the members participate; the homonoia of the members, their likemindedness through the Spirit that has become flesh in all and each of them, welds them into a universal community of mankind" (ER, 95-96). The source of the community, the Spirit, is transcendentally out of time so that it can be universally present in time and constitute thereby the image of mankind as a universal community. What replaced the image of mankind in the Christian sense varied according to the preferences of intellectuals: in all cases, however, the result was useful in that the new communities were organized into highly efficient task-forces.

The great pragmatic difficulty is that immature and fragmentary images of a reduced human being do not alter the reality of one's humanity. Thus, when real difficulties arise, they cannot be understood in their proper amplitude but are interpreted by way of the categories of the new anthropology. But since action was originally undertaken to realize the image expressed in these categories, more of the same can only make matters worse, and, unless one has lost touch with reality completely, the disproportion between the inadequate imagery and the genuinely unsatisfactory state of affairs will be expressed by highly unstable moods ranging from quite specific hatreds and obsessions (Jews, Pakistanis, bankers, intellectuals, Southerners, Texans, hippies, etc.) to vague insecurities, fears, and anxieties (something is wrong with the world, the system, the university, ...etc.), often accompanied by appropriately specific or vague magical solutions. Now, it is not impossible to pierce these anxieties and show that they stem from a refusal to develop one's personality beyond the level that allowed one to indulge in this exquisite game, that the game itself attempts to circumvent the mystery, that the person who does so favor his phantasy prefers, to use one of Voegelin's later formulae, certain untruth to uncertain truth --but, prior to undertaking an analysis of the state of consciousness involved, the individual must be moved by an appeal, which is pre-analytic, to a change of heart. There is no reason to be sanguine about the probability of a successful appeal. As George

Grant remarked, to think outside the faith of North America moving forward in expansionist practicality "is to make oneself a stranger to the public realm."[25]

*

This chapter has been focally concerned with Voegelin's analysis of the spiritual crisis of Western society and the interpretative principles used to conduct the analysis. Consequently, it has not been possible to illustrate the most useful and impressive aspect of the book, namely the wealth of reasoned and detailed exposition. Secondly, the analysis provided so far has deliberately concentrated on the material dealing with political ideas prior to the French Revolution. One reason for this focus was to emphasize that the new complex of sentiments and ideas was not just a French affair but, on the contrary, is a common Western movement, the differential impact of which may be traced to the dampening effects of political institutions and the degree of persistence of preexisting social and religious substance, discussed in the first part of the chapter. One of the great services that Voegelin's book performed, therefore, was to bring to light, when they were still young and audacious, the spiritual processes that later simmered down into the conventional banalities of contemporary political chatter. The danger with focussing on the pre-Revolutionary people is that one may consider political opinion after the French Revolution simply as a continuation of the progressive movement. There were, of course, continuities; but, mindful of the link between political history and political thought, we are sensitive to the fact that the sheer event of the Revolution had its own impact.

At the risk of being over-schematic, one may divide the post-Revolutionary period, from the death of Condorcet in 1794 to the death of Marx in 1883, into three phases. First is the phase of vulgarization and dissemination of already debased opinions; secondly, the search for, and establishment of, new religions; thirdly, a phase of demonic revolt against the shadow of stable spirituality contained in the new religions. The later phases are distinctive for their additions to the earlier ones, which they took as starting points. Thus we find in Marx, for example, a sophistic vulgarity fully equal to that of Condorcet.

When Kant asked his famous "Was ist Aufklaerung?" he did not foresee its end product, the "naive dogmatism" (ER, 125) of a Condorcet. Yet, to employ the Platonic image once again, if education towards the realissimum is symbolized by the long struggle from cave to sunlight, surely one could anticipate the results of trying to bring the light below: whether a torch or a portable generator is used, soon enough the entire cave is filled with noxious fumes and nobody can see the way out. In any case, publicists such as Condorcet can serve as no more than warning examples of intellectuals who seek to control the destiny of the rest of humanity by regularizing behaviour according to probabilistic laws.

With Comte, who had lived through the Revolution, a new phase began. In the aftermath of the failure of the attempt at establishing "a caesaropapistic regime of a non-Christian religion" (ER, 171) the question of the spiritual reintegration of society became a central focus not only for Comte, Saint-Simon, and the other "prophets of Paris," as Manuel has called the collection, but also for the so-called reactionaries and liberals. The French Revolution revealed clearly for the first time "that the apocalypse of man is driving, by the logic of sentiment, toward the deification of intramundane society. The Revolution has been carried by its momentum beyond the peripheral questions of governmental form to the very heart of the crisis, that is, to the destruction of Western Christian civilization and to the tentative creation of a non-Christian society" (ER, 176). The creation of programmes to stabilize the revolutionary movement by imposing the contours of a particular vision on everyone else as the new order of society petered out with the passing of the generation that had lived through the Revolution. With the generation of Bakunin and Marx problems of religious foundation were replaced by an activist mysticism blazing with eschatalogical fervor.

On the over one hundred pages of text devoted to what is arguably the best short analysis of Bakunin and Marx in existence, we will permit ourselves but two remarks. Voegelin opened the first chapter on Bakunin with the sentence: "In the life of Michael Bakunin (1814-76) depths of Satanism and nihilism become visible which in the life and work of other great figures of the Western crisis are covered over by remnants of traditional order and by veils of futuristic planning" (ER, 195). Since "the system of Marx would never have been

written and never exerted its influence unless it had
originated in the genuine pathos of revolutionary existence that we find in its purity in Bakunin" (ER, 201),
it is important to clarify precisely what is "Satanic"
about these two. The first level of meaning is provided
by Bakunin himself in his version of the Fall as told
in Genesis. God prohibited man from tasting of the
Tree of Knowledge because He wanted man to remain an
animal; but Satan, "the emancipator of the world" shames
man for his ignorance and emancipates him by persuading
him to eat, and begin the specifically human development
in revolt towards knowledge (ER, 237-238). As Satan in
the Biblical story, so man, according to Bakunin, is
defined by revolt.

With Marx this self-conscious Satanism of revolt
took on an additional feature. Marx, like Bakunin, was
an activist mystic, aware of the crisis of the epoch
and ready with a solution to it in the form of the
Revolution that changes the heart of man. But, if the
sought-for Revolution ever did take place, the heart of
man would not change and the new world would be as
unsatisfactory as the old one. This typical impasse of
activist mysticism was met by Marx in the following
way: unlike other sectarians who created the chosen
ones before setting them loose on the destructive-creative
task of revolution, Marx felt that the Revolution itself
would produce the chosen ones. In this way his mysticism
was even more impervious to common sense than Bakunin's
lust for destruction: the Revolution would have to occur
before his opinion could be tested, and even if, following
a vast social upheaval, the new world was not created,

this could only mean that these events were not the
real Revolution. And since no actual upheaval in the
real world will ever achieve anything in the mystic
dream-world, politics becomes exhaustively defined as
tactics, and Marx's rebelliousness becomes
indistinguishable from Bakunin's. The common Satanism
of Bakunin and Marx, then, consists in an endless revolt
against whatever social order achieves institutional stability, "a mobilization scheme for warfare without the
end of peace."[26] The new regime of endless mobilization,
which Arendt has analyzed as being at the heart of
totalitarianism, is adequately described by the language
of Satanism.

*

Most readers of From Enlightenment to Revolution
will understand easily enough the critical exuberance
of the book although the "dead end" to which this criticism
led will be less apparent. Voegelin himself was aware
of the irresponsible side of critical analysis: "the
purpose of criticism is, of course, not to prove a proposi-
tion wrong and to let it go at that, but to clarify, by
means of criticism the insight into the problem that
has found an unsatisfactory formulation" (ER, 37 fn.
7). One meets, therefore, the problem of critical dissolution by the positive insights that one gains: there is
a via negativa in discursive theory as well as in theology.
Yet, the comparative primitiveness of Voegelin's vocabulary in this book is clear to all who know his later
work. Paying due regard to the question of compactness
and differentiation with respect to Voegelin's terminolo-

gy, one may venture to conclude that From Enlightenment to Revolution displays a portion of the empirical evidence for Voegelin's theoretical insights that only later attained an unambiguously adequate conceptual form. In the following chapter we discuss one of the most significant reformulations in Voegelin's political philosophy, the discovery and elaboration of the concept of historiogenesis.

NOTES

[1]
Voegelin discussed neither the fine arts nor Hegel
here. He has explained (in the Journal of the American Academy of Religion, 43 (1975), pp. 767-77) why it
took him so long to come to terms with Hegel and
published a major article on Hegel only in 1971 ("On
Hegel: A Study in Sorcery.") Voegelin's article,
"Nietzsche, the Crisis and the War," reflected the
date of its composition (1944), though its fundamental
analyses could easily serve wider purposes.

[2]
"Siger de Brabant;" "Bakunin's Confession;" "Plato's
Egyptian Myth;" "The Origins of Scientism;" "The
Philosophy of Existence: Plato's Gorgias;" "The
Formation of the Marxian Revolutionary Idea;"
"Machiavelli's Prince: Background and Formation;"
"More's Utopia." In addition, one may mention "Das
Timurbild der Humanisten: Eine Studie zur politischen
Mythenbildung," parts of which were incorporated in
the article on Machiavelli.

[3]
The other great insight of this period, the development of a theory of consciousness, grew out of
Voegelin's discussions and correspondence with Alfred
Schutz. Part I of Voegelin's Anamnesis provides some
of the details of this development. It is discussed
below in Chapter Six. In this chapter we shall employ
Voegelin's earlier vocabulary, with its conventional
and, to some extent, uncritical terminology. Thus,
for example, Voegelin could write of the "system" of
St. Thomas or of Plato whereas later he remarked that
to apply as a philosophical term the word "system" to
any thinker before Descartes was an anachronism, and
afterwards it was no longer philosophical but gnostic
(SPG, 42-3).

[4]
In the absence of any detailed analysis of Voegelin's
several prewar books and articles we are making the
entirely unjustified but, at present, necessary
assumption that the period before the History is a

kind of prehistory. As we mentioned above in Chapter One, it was a period of formation and resistance both to political events and to the inadequacies of current interpretations of those events.

[5] OH IV, 57 See below, Chapter Four for further discussion of this question.

[6] "Configurations in History," 42.

[7] "Political Theory and the Pattern of General History;" subsequent quotes are from this article.

[8] In the second part of the article Voegelin elaborated six areas where, following the principle that the history of political theory must be subordinate to the empirical structure of political history, the historian of political theory "has the fascinating opportunity" of trying to integrate "a wealth of monographic studies on special phases of political theory" with "a knowledge of political history far surpassing the knowledge of a generation ago." The History, including From Enlightenment to Revolution, attempted precisely to bring these two complexes of knowledge together.

[9] "The Growth of the Race Idea; subsequent quotations are taken from pp. 283-286. The earlier work is contained in Rasse und Statt (Tubingen: J.C.B. Mohr, 1933) and Die Rassenidee in der Geistesgeschichte von Ray bis Carus, (Berlien: Junker und Dunnhaupt, 1933).

[10] A brief statement of Scheler's argument in English is his Man's Place in Nature, tr. with an intro. by Hans Meyerhoff, (Boston: Beacon Press, 1961).

[11] "The Theory of Legal Science: A Review;" all quotations are from pp. 560-563.

[12] Those familiar only with Voegelin's New Science of Politics, which is probably his most widely read book

(9th printing, 1974), will recognize an early formulation of the topic of Chapter III of that work, "representation and truth." On another occasion, Voegelin was even more straightforward and plain-spoken: "by analysis I mean that we approach any study of society from the standpoint of the opinions of those around us. We find in our immediate circle both the opinions and the terminology expressing ideas of right or wrong; our job as political scientists is to find the path leading from this vocabulary and those customs toward the objective element. This is introduced by the postulate that there is such a thing as human nature, and if we can discover what it consists of we can offer advice as to how society ought to be organized, since the organization of society should aim at the full flowering of human nature. . . thus the focal point of political science should always be what today we call philosophical anthropology, which in fact corresponds to the first chapter of the Nichomachean Ethics." "Industrial Society in Search of Reason," 223-224.

13 These answers would appear incomplete today in a rhetorical, if not a theoretical, sense because they tend to over-estimate the persuasive power of rational discussion in bringing about the "convergence." Consider, for example, Voegelin's remarks in the following articles: "On Readiness to Rational Discussion," "On Debate and Existence," and "The Eclipse of Reality."

14 "The Growth of the Race Idea," 313.

15 "The Oxford Political Philosophers," 100.

16 op. cit., 104. Consider in this respect the reply of J.D. Mabbot, "Note on 'The Oxford Political Philosophers,'" The Philosophical Quarterly., 4 (1954), 258-261.

17 "The Oxford Political Philosophers," 114.

18 The aftermath of the Western presence in India is in some contrast with the results left in China. In part this is doubtless a reflection of indigenous factors, but in part, too, it reflects a somewhat richer mixture of political ideas informing a more moderate British Imperial practice in the Indian sub-continent (a desire for loot plus a sense of "civilizing" duty, which introduced such notions as the rule of law, parliamentary government, etc.) as distinct from the general Western pillage of China.

19 Voegelin's account of Turgot emphasized his historicism as a component of the larger complex of ideas and sentiments that crystallized in the positivist movement. Our analysis here stresses Turgot's importance for the development of Voegelin's account.

20 By "substance" Voegelin meant (at least with regard to politics) "the Koine common reality in which communities of men could express the identity of the ground in themselves with the ground in the universe" (ER, 116).

21 To take an an example from Voegelin's recent work: the imagery of a genealogical descent from Adam and Shem in the Biblical P-text is experientially equivalent to the Hesiodic symbolism of world Ages as well as to the story of the Fall in the Biblical J-text. In conceptual summary, one element in the reality experienced in-dwelling in these various imageries, is that human existence in time is imperfect. See OH, IV, 82-90. See also Voegelin's analysis of the experiences of seeking (zetein) and drawing (helkein) in classical philosophy and the Gospel, in "The Gospel and Culture." On Shelling, see also Anamnesis, 50-54. Voegelin provided twenty anamnetic sketches of formative childhood experiences in Anamnesis, 61-76.

22 "Normally the past and the future are present; we do not stand between them, but are moving in the

continous stream of history. The past reaches into
our present as the civilization heritage that has
formed us and that we absorb into our lives as the
precondition for the formation of the future, not in
some distant time ahead of us, but in the present of
our daily life and work." "The Theory of Legal
Science," 568.

[23] Consider also Voegelin's remarks on the
"'stop-history' movement" in OH, IV, 331-333.

[24] "Immortality: "Experience and Symbol," 238.

[25] "In Defence of North America" in Technology and Empire
(Toronto: Anansi, 1969), 28.

[26] Gerhart Niemeyer, Between Nothingness and Paradise,
(Baton Rouge: Louisiana State University Press,
1971), 125. Niemeyer was speaking of Lenin; his
remark applies equally to Bakunin and Marx. Consider
Voegelin's later remarks on Satanism in "The Turn of
The Screw," 32 and "The Gospel and Culture," 95-96.

CHAPTER FOUR

THE CONCEPT OF HISTORIOGENESIS

Several years ago Karl Loewith reminded his readers that the advent of the "philosophy of history," marked a watershed in European thought: "The inauguration of the philosophy of history was an emancipation from the theological interpretation and antireligious in principle."[1] It is, perhaps, a mark of our secular and enlightened era that we presently employ the term seemingly in innocence of its polemical past. We are likely to look upon Voltaire's squabble with Bossuet essentially as a conflict between philosophies of history, one Christian, one not. Nor are we wholly wrong to do so, though we court the danger of misunderstanding what the controversy was all about unless we introduce suitable qualifications. One of these would be that,(beneath their quarrels concerning the principle and methods of historical interpretation), was a substantial dispute that focussed on what we would call a philosophy of historical existence. What separated Voltaire and his successors from Bossuet and his, concerned the structure of human being, the nature of human reason and the modes of human participation in the several orders of being. As was indicated in the last chapter, the course from enlightenment to revolution was, according to Voegelin, the story of the genesis of modern, Western unreason. And Western unreason lies at the heart of what is indicated by the term crisis of European and now ecumenic consciousness.

One of Voegelin's achievements is to have made thematic the issue that lies at the origin of this crisis. In this respect one may say he continued the work of Paul Hazard's The Crisis of European Consciousness (1935). Competent judges of Voegelin's multivolume Order and History have nearly all been lavish in their praise of his work, which combines a vast historical erudition with profound philosophical insight. Here the work of Hazard's great contemporary Henri Bergson, especially his Two Sources of Mortality and Religion (1932) may be suggested as being of comparable richness. The topic of the present chapter, the concept of historiogenesis, illustrates well both aspects of Voegelin's work. The term itself was introduced by Voegelin in 1960 in an article published in German and almost simultaneously printed in a Festschrift honouring a colleague, Alois Dempf. A second version appeared in his book, Anamnesis, published in 1966, and the final and definitive version is Chapter One of Volume IV of Order and History, published late in 1974. The concept has not, however, received much attention from historians, philosophers or political scientists.

There may be several reasons for this, but one of them is likely to be the complexity and subtlety of the concept. Voegelin has several times indicated that it is methodologically inappropriate simply to agree upon a definition and then proceed to use it as a conceptual sabre to slash apart large blocks of historical evidence or trim them to fit the contours of a definition. Voegelin's conceptual apparatus was deeply embedded in empirical evidence, and did not lend itself easily to an abstract presentation. Moreover, his argument was terse and often employed a specialized terminology. This means that a faithful exegesis of the concept that is the present topic would be considerably longer than the sixty-five pages of text Voegelin devoted to his own elaboration. Any representation would, therefore, take much longer than the present occasion could accommodate. Worse yet, much of the material that Voegelin introduced as evidence is unfamiliar. One cannot simply allude to the Sumerian King List or an Egyptian funereal text the way one might allude to the Treaty of Utrecht, Plato's philosopher-king, or Rousseau's social contract. Accordingly, we shall suggest by a few examples the richness of his analysis. Possibly the most serious problem for Voegelin's readers concerns neither his vocabulary nor the range of evidence he drew upon; both of these difficulties are essentially technical in nature and can be mastered by the assiduous application of intelligence. The most serious problem, rather, concerns Voegelin's understanding of political philosophy.

Readers of Voegelin's book on Plato and Aristotle will recall his insistence that philosophy is an act of resistance to that spiritual corruption whose political manifestation is injustice. In The New Science of Politics, under the heading of gnosticism, Voegelin analyzed the characteristically modern disturbances of spiritual order. His more recent work has been devoted to a problem common to both The New Science of Politics and the early volumes of Order and History but not treated thematically in either, namely, the dogmatization of symbols and antidogmatic reaction. The specific aspect

of the combat situation, as Voegelin has called it,
that is of present interest is suggested by a passage
in Anamnesis where he reflected upon what he called the
corruption or degradation of myth: "The mediative myths
of the Christian tradition are decomposing for ever larger
masses of people. The spiritualized expressions of the
experience of transcendence in intellectual mysticism
and philosophical speculation are available only to a
small minority. The inevitable result is the appearance
of 'lostness' in a world that no longer has a centre of
order in myth" (Anam., 50). Having lost touch with
order or cosmos through the medium of myth, modern human
beings have sought refuge in acosmic or anticosmic myths
and doctrinal systems that do no more than express their
present alienation. As George Grant once put it, "one
can find no fulfillment in working for, or celebrating,
the dynamo."2 One of Voegelin's purposes, then, was to
recover the meaning of cosmos through an exegesis of
the experiential reality that we moderns have taken such
care to avoid.

The corruption of popular myth is balanced, among
the learned, by an equally degraded understanding of
political philosophy or political theory. In The New
Science of Politics Voegelin remarked: "Theory is not
just any opining about human existence in society; it
rather is an attempt at formulating the meaning of existence by explicating the content of a definite class of
experiences." Furthermore, he said, the validity of a
theoretical argument "derives...from the aggregate of
experiences to which it must permanently refer for empirical control" (NSP, 64). Very well, it may be objected,

but precisely <u>what</u> experiences are involved? In <u>The</u>
<u>New</u> <u>Science</u>, Voegelin referred to the example of the
Aristotelian <u>spoudaios</u> (<u>E.N.</u>, 1113a 29 ff) as one who
"judges all things rightly, what they truly are as they
appear to him" because he is himself "the standard and
measure" of what is noble and truly eudaimonic. There
are difficulties in Aristotle's theory of man, not the
least of which concerns the rhetoric of its presentation,
and we shall consider shortly Voegelin's way of dealing
with them. What nevertheless has been secured by the
reference to Aristotle is this: theoretical experience
is a reality in the inner life of a person whose character
is formed, precisely, by what is noble and truly
eudaimonic. Corresponding to this inner or personal
reality is the outer or public exegesis and explication
of it. That is, Voegelin (and Aristotle) would insist
that the familiar, public side to theory or philosophy
is essentially derivative.

We may generalize the question even further, and
consider explicitly a topic to which reference has been
made more than once, namely, the distinction between
symbolism and dogmatism. Symbols are language terms
engendered from experience and developed with the intention of conveying meaning. Some experience is, for example, perceptual, and is adequately presented by the
description of phenomena. In addition, however, one
experiences non-phenomenal meaning, meaning that need
not appear phenomenally or for which phenomenality is
an accidental and transparent contingency. The Canadian
flag, for example, is more than a stylized public botanical
study; it points beyond what appears to another meaning.

As Voegelin wrote in The New Science, human society is composed of both an external or phenomenal aspect and an internal aspect of meaning: "it is a whole, a little world, a cosmion, illuminated with meaning from within by the human beings who continuously create and bear it as the mode and condition of their self-realization" (NSP, 27). Society as cosmion is luminous with meaning insofar as the symbols that are its internal constitution express through their structure the universal meaning that is the mystery of human existence. As we shall see below, this statement carries with it the twofold implication that, qua mystery, human experience can never be fully articulate, though we may distinguish more and less adequate symbolic expressions of it. Secondly, qua universal meaning, one can speak of distinct but equivalent symbolisms insofar as different language terms may be advanced to refer to the same experienced reality --which we have just referred to as the mystery of existence.

The relationship between symbols and human beings is reciprocal: on the one hand, human beings express their experience of self-realization by means of symbols --one can conceive, for example, of people less spiritually sensitive than George Grant for whom service to the dynamo is a supreme act of fulfillment. On the other hand, symbols express to reflective consciousness, including that of the philosopher, political scientist and historian, the experience that one is fully human only by virtue of participation in a whole that transcends one's particular existence. As Voegelin said on the opening page of Order and History: "The perspective of participation must be understood in the fullness of its disturbing quality... Participation in being...is not a partial involvement of man; he is engaged with the whole of his existence, for participation is existence itself" (OH, I:1). However disturbing and ultimately mysterious existence may be, it is neither experienced as a monism of anxiety nor is it understood, by analogy with sight, as being utterly opaque. Symbols illuminate the experience of participation more or less adequately according to one's intentions and powers of discrimination and articulation. However, there can be no guarantee that the intended meaning will be reconstituted in the consciousness of a reader or hearer because there is no authoritative perspective or vantage point outside existence from which the meaning of the whole could be captured in an unambiguous and final form.

We may conclude, therefore, that the substratum of the experience of participation, that is, of existence, is a constant process that from any particular point of place or time appears to be vanishing. With the best intentions and the greatest powers of discrimination and articulation, all one can do is create symbols that exist as a kind of worldly residue. Once created, however, these symbols can be understood independently of the occasion of their creation; they are but language terms and as Plato once remarked in a similar context, unable to defend themselves against misunderstandings (Phaedrus, 275c-e). Nevertheless, "the truth conveyed by symbols...is the source of right order in human existence; we cannot dispense with it; and, as a consequence, the pressure is great to restate the exegetic account discursively for the purpose of communication."[3] The discursive, conceptual presentation of the experience of participation results in a dogmatic or doctrinal mode of discourse.

The transformation of symbolism into dogmatism is not confined to what we may loosely term "religious experience." Plato's objection to the Homeric epic, for example, was conditioned by the altered meaning of mythopoesis: the *Iliad* and the *Odyssey* were no longer understood symbolically, as the expression of the crisis of Achaean society, but literally, as collections of maxims, tales of adventure, and naughty stories about gods. The transition from classical to Stoic philosophy was likewise a process of increasing opacity. Where Socrates enacted a life of wondering, searching, love, hope, faith, a "theoretical life" in the sense that Voegelin used the word, and Plato and Aristotle employed these concrete terms in order to describe their own actual and meditative reenactment of this philosophical life, the Stoics developed an abstract term, *tasis*, tension, to indicate a property of the psyche, now conceived as a phenomenal thing. Accordingly they spoke of the tension of existence where Plato explored meditatively its modes as love, hope, searching etc., and Socrates experienced immediately his existence in terms of the descriptive terms employed by Plato. The procedure in general may be summarized as follows: first, symbols, whether mythopoetic or philosophical, are literalized into abstract concepts, propositions, and doctrines; and second, doctrinal terms are reinterpreted allegorically and imaginatively.

The allegorical interpretation of doctrine necessarily deforms the experiential meaning of symbols. Even so, doctrine has served the quite positive purpose, under the Ciceronian category "religion," of protecting the spiritual insights of philosophy from the disintegrative turmoil of society. In a like fashion, Jewish and Christian scripture and dogma have served as protective devices for the confessional life of the community of believers. In the present age, however, "the deforming doctrinalization has become socially stronger than the experiential insights it was originally meant to protect" (OH, IV, 58). The task of the historian or political philosopher, aware of what has happened, is therefore delicate indeed. "On the one hand, he is not permitted to side with the believers and, in particular, he must not let himself be betrayed into arguing...doctrinal questions such as whether man, or his soul, is immortal or not," but on the other, "he is not permitted to side with the objectors, as they deny validity to propositions concerning God, the Soul, and Immortality, on the ground that they cannot be verified or falsified like propositions concerning objects of sense-perception." Treading a narrow line between the contestants, one "must grant the intellectual advantage to the objector, because he escapes the believer's fallacy of operating with hypostatized symbols," but at the same time, one "must grant the existential advantage to the believer, because the objector pays for his intellectual cleanliness the price of denying truth altogether, while the believer preserves truth experienced at least in its doctrinal derivation."4 In terms of interpretative strategy, Voegelin indicated that a dialectical balance between scientific suspicion and participatory trust is required for any adequate discussion of experience and symbolization.

*

We are now in a position to discuss directly Voegelin's concept, historiogenesis. This initial discussion of symbolism and dogmatism was a necessary prelude: just as the meaning of Homeric epic or Platonic philosophy has been subject to successive transformation, so too has the symbolism of historiogenesis been deformed into doctrine and ideology. Voegelin's concept refers to "a particular type of speculation on the order of society, its origin, and its course in time" whereby governance springs into existence "at an absolute point of origin, as part of the cosmic order itself, and from that point down they i.e., the symbolists who develop this type of speculation, let the history of their society descend to the present in which they live" (OH, IV, 59). Formally, historiogenetic speculation may be divided into two parts: events falling within the lifetime of the contemporary generation or one or two generations earlier, and mythical events that are linked, through an act of mythopoesis, to the emergence of cosmic order. Because recent events can be tied back in time to the establishment of the cosmos, they are deemed worthy of being passed on to future generations.

The earliest evidence Voegelin adduced was from the third millennium B.C., over 4,000 years ago, in the empires of the ancient near east. That is, contrary to our conventional wisdom, "pagans" and "Gentiles" not

Israelites and Christians, were the first to develop a notion of history as a meaningful course of events organized on a straight line of time. The reworking of the near eastern materials as a result of dissatisfaction with the results in the first volume of Order and History led to the formulation of the concept of historiogenesis. Voegelin then had to reconsider this same evidence, including Israelite and Christian texts, in light of the new insight. This working out of the interpretative dialectic, along with administrative duties, was a major reason for the seventeen year gap between the publication of Volumes III and IV of Order and History. That is, Voegelin qualified in Volume IV the magisterial words that opened the Preface to his study: "The order of history emerges from the history of order." He did not, however, disavow the equally magisterial words of his Introduction: "God and man, world and society, form a primordial community of being" (OH, I, ix, 1). Indeed, one can see from the perspective opened by Volume IV that historiogenesis was already implied in the formula "God and man, world and society."

Historiogenesis is a speculation on the origin and cause of social order, a "quest for the ground" of being. In this respect it is one of a class of symbolisms that include theogeny, anthropogeny and cosmogeny, with the difference that the focus of participation in the primordial community of being has shifted from the divine, human, and cosmic aspects, considered in the first three volumes of Order and History, to the social. That is, the motive for historiogenesis must be sought within the experience of history in the pragmatic sense of what happens to a concrete society. First of all, society must have existed for a sufficiently long time that a retrospective extrapolation of events to an absolute starting point is persuasive. Social stability, however, is never absolute: a second motive, thus, may be sought in the anxiety induced by a threat to the stability, and more radically, to the existence, of a society.

The imperial societies of the ancient near east developed an elaborate symbolism to express and thereby come to terms with such a threat. New Year rituals, for example, annually renewed the order of society by an analogical repetition of the original creation of the cosmos. Historiogenetic speculation, on the other hand, "implacably places events on a line of irreversible time where opportunities are lost forever and defeat is final" OH, IV, 79). Accordingly, a careful examination of the origin of the symbolism of cyclical, or more adequately, rhythmical, time brings to light the problem of cosmic lasting. In this connection it has been argued that Mesopotamian myths of cosmic renewal following upon cosmic catastrophe were developed as responses to the celestial precession of the equinoxes through the zodiac.[5] The primary experience of the cosmos, therefore, was one of instability as well as stability. The time of the cosmic cycles, as distinct from the time of the cosmos that constitutes the cycles, was not afflicted with this instability. As we discuss in more detail in chapter five, one may speak of a hierarchy of lasting, from the time of an individual, to that of his society, to the cosmos, and finally to the sempiternal time of the cycles.

Speculation on the time of the cycles is, in effect, speculation on the entire temporal course of the cosmos. We have already noted a formal division of historiogenesis into two segments of quite unequal duration. The shorter is an account of recent events experienced or remembered; the longer traces the remembered events back to the origin of the cosmos by way of mythopoetic discourse. Let us consider the specific example of the Sumerian King List. The so-called Sumerian Empire was a collection of cities united from time to time under an hegemonic city. The history of the Sumerian Empire is, therefore, the story of the several cities existing for their spans of time as subjects or rulers. The authors of the King List, however, placed the dynastic histories of the various cities on a single time-line of succession issuing in their own present. "The parallel histories of the cities were abolished, but nevertheless absorbed into an imaginary unilinear history of empire. One cosmos, it appears, can have only one imperial order, and the sin of coexistence must be atoned by posthumous integration into the one history whose goal has been demonstrated by the success of the conqueror" (OH, IV, 65). The only society that really mattered was the last one.

The fictitious succession was extended back beyond the first actual dynasty, through legendary materials, to a Great Flood, and then to five antediluvian dynasties. There were eight kings before the flood, with a total reign of about 241,000 years; the first dynasty after the flood reigned for about 24,500 years and the second, before the reign of historically plausible individual kings who were said to continue it, 2,300 years. Voegelin has suggested that the construction of the periods was based on a principle of numerical speculation that attempted to integrate the mythical succession of kings with the empirically observed precession of the equinoxes.

Before suggesting what this may mean let us consider a more familiar example. In the genealogical successions preserved in the Book of Genesis, descendants of Adam live between 700 and 1,000 years; the descendants of Shem, 200 to 600 years; the patriarchs live between 100 and 200 years, and ordinary men, 70 to 80 years. The longevity of these predecessors to ordinary humans has occasioned a good deal of commentary since the Bible has, until recently, been understood as a truthful and literal account of human history. Contemporary Old Testament scholars take a somewhat different approach. On various philological grounds, they distinguish several literary traditions that have been combined as the Biblical text. Gerhart von Rad, for example, has pointed out that the P or priestly document that contains the genealogical tables does not contain a story of the Fall; he suggested that the declining ages of the several categories of people may be understood as a symbolical representation of an increasing distance from the miraculous and superabundant vitality present at the origin of creation. Voegelin added to von Rad's insight that the story of the Fall in the J or Yahwist document "makes the expression by means of periods of declining vitality superfluous. Hence, the story of the Fall must be recognized as expressing, alternative to the speculation on periods, the experience of a tension between the destiny of man and his temporal status" (OH, IV, 89). The story of the Fall, therefore, is equivalent in meaning not only to the genealogical speculation of the Biblical P-document but also to the Sumerian speculation on the harmony of the zodiac and the descent of dynasties. The constant motive for historiogenetic speculation, then, is the experience that existence in time is imperfect.

If all that were involved with historiogenesis was the experience of imperfection in existence, one would expect that the story of the Fall would have definitively superseded it. Firstly, the story of the Fall removed the awkwardness associated with thousand-year old Adamites and two hundred-year old patriarchs. The Fall occurs once for all: it touches every individual in his or her personal life without any mediation through membership in a collective. But historiogenesis persists in spite of the apparent superiority of the story of Adam and Eve. Indeed, Voegelin said, it "even displays a tendency to swallow up all other types of mytho-speculation. It is the symbolism by which the cosmological style of truth survives most obdurately in social fields whose style of truth is informed by philosophy and revelation" (OH, IV: 91). That is to say, historiogenetic speculation survives with undiminished vigor into classical, medieval, and modern western societies. The strength of the story of the Fall, namely its immediacy, is also its weakness insofar as it does not shed much light upon the sufferings of collective political disruptions and conquest nor, more generally, on the social dimension of existence. Historiogenetic speculation meets this deficiency.

In the first volume of Order and History Voegelin analyzed Israelite theophantic experience and its symbolization as the history of the Chosen People of Yahweh. The aspect of his account of interest here is what he called the "perpetual mortgage of the world-immanent, concrete event on the transcendent truth that on its occasion was revealed" (OH, I, 164). The imagery of a mortgage was intended to indicate the disproportion between the experience of the revelation of God's way with human beings, the "transcendent truth" to be lived in obedience to Yahweh's instructions, and the pragmatic expression it attained within the comparatively insignificant political and ethnic community of the Israelites and later in the still small but pragmatically more successful Kingdoms. One expression of this disproportion was found in the opposition of the prophets. In Voegelin's words, "it required the efforts of a whole galaxy of Prophets to differentiate the spiritual meaning of Yahwism from a symbolism that enclosed it compactly in the ordering instructions for an association of nomad clans. And once these efforts had achieved a certain measure of success, the oppositional character of Prophetism had become doubly futile. For, pragmatically, the opposition had lost its target with the destruction of the Kingdoms; and, spiritually, it became obvious that the existence or nonexistence of a Kingdom of Israel was irrelevant for the fundamental problems of a life in righteousness before the Lord" (OH, I, 182). This same "mortgage" is apparent within the historiogenetic symbolic form.

In Volume IV of <u>Order</u> <u>and</u> <u>History</u> Voegelin described the problem as follows: "Through the Sinai event, man has acquired his consciousness of historical immediacy under God. The new insight, however, did not dissolve historiogenesis but, on the contrary, was absorbed into its symbolism. Historical consciousness, though its meaning was clear to the prophets, did not gain its full organizing force in the elaboration of symbols but had to submit to historiogenetic speculation of the cosmological type" (<u>OH</u>, IV, 97). Now, we know from the exegesis of Exodus provided by Volume I, that Egypt, the house of institutional bondage where the Israelites were employed in public works, became Egypt, the house of spiritual death, Sheol (<u>OH</u>, I, 112). The establishment of the kingdom was, in these terms, a reversal of the Exodus, a re-entry into Sheol <u>OH</u>, I, 142). The Prophetic resistance to the "yoke of historiogenesis" (<u>OH</u>, IV, 99) was likewise an attempt to elaborate the universalist potentiality of Yahwism. This meant a prophetic re-exodus not from Egypt but from the kingdom, the meaning of which was sustained and buttressed by historiogenetic stories.

The task was not an easy one. We know, however, from the example of Hellenic historiogenesis, that it was not dependent on the institution of an empire or kingdom. The great importance of imperial institutions was that they provided a repository for annals and records to preserve facts and dates. Owing to lack of annalistic sources, Hellenic historiogenesis moved rapidly from a brief historical narrative through mythical events to an absolute origin. In the absence of an imperial society to act as an incarnate vessel of historiogenetic meaning, speculation was free to expand to the empirically known mankind. The vast sweep of Herodotus's survey of the ecumene, the known world, and the nomoi, the traditions and customs of its inhabitants, contrasts sharply with the brevity of his five paragraph account of the prehistory of the Persian Wars. Moreover, the Hellenic historians preserved the sense of a common historical drama by organizing their materials according to philosophical hypothesis, which meant that they could abandon the imagery of gods jolting the whole process into motion.[6] Indeed, Herodotus transformed mythical events, the successive rapes of Io, Europa, Medea, and Helen into a series of historical events that nicely balanced one another. Benardete has shown, furthermore, that this Anaximandrian concern for "paying the penalty and compensation to one another" extends to the topical structure of Herodotus' great inquiry.[7] Hellenic historiogenesis, in short, was able, in principle, to accommodate an ecumenic mankind as the carrier of historiogenetic meaning. This insight, so far as it goes, could not, and cannot, be superseded.

Let us gather together the threads of the argument thus far. Historiogenesis is a mytho-speculative extrapolation of pragmatic history towards its cosmic-divine originating point. It need not start from an imperial present, as the Hellenic evidence indicated, though there are sound organizational as well as political reasons why it might. The elasticity of the symbolism no less than its durability reflect the reality of the primary experience of the cosmos. The differentiation of consciousness, symbolized for example by a world-transcendent

God, does not abolish the primary experience. In Voegelin's words: "By virtue of a revelatory experience of man's existence in society, its time dimension may be recognized as the history that is transparent for divine order; by virtue of noetic insight, the problem of beginning and end may be recognized as an antinomy attaching to the flux of time; but neither revelation nor philosophy dissolve time and the tale of the cosmos" (OH, IV, 101). In the example of Herodotus, despite the Anaximandrian noetic structure, the motivation for the work was clearly the precariousness of Hellenic power restored at the battles of Marathon and Salamis. The Persian Wars, that is, were understood as a disturbance of ecumenic not parochial Greek or Asiatic order. The same ecumenic sentiment was present in Aeschylus' The Persians, which presented defeat as a tragic fall from greatness. In neither instance, however, did the time-horizon extend more than a couple of generations. In the Timaeus (22b), Plato had the Egyptian priest inform Solon that the Hellenes were children: "there is no such thing as an old Hellene." Nevertheless, the absence of an imperial organization and Hellenic "youth" did not inhibit Hellenic historiogenetic speculation. On the contrary, the blending of noetic symbolism, of philosophy or "theory," to use Voegelin's earlier language, with an experience of historical precariousness led to speculation on the nature of man and the possibility that mankind was the bearer of that nature.

The dogmatization of historiogenetic speculation, to which Voegelin gave the name historiomachy, consisted, during the period of ecumenic empires beginning with

Alexander, of historiographic competition by several rival authors each of whom claimed to have written a universal history of mankind. In this competition the Orientals, with their enormous archival deposits were at a great advantage over the Hellenic children. A comic illustration of this dogmatization may be found in the Stromateis of Clement of Alexandria (I, 101-47). Here Clement claimed superiority for Christianity by comparing the dates of Prometheus, Isis, Demeter, Apollo and so on, with Moses and Solomon. The Hellenic gods were turned into comparatively recent historical personages and given their assigned place on a single line of time centered on the birth of Christ. In summarizing this tendency of historiogenetic speculation to absorb or swallow alternative theogenic, authropogenic and cosmogenic accounts, Voegelin remarked, "the symbols of the theogenic etc. myth have their truth as an analogy of being; if this consciousness of analogical truth is now destroyed, one of the principle causes (there were others) must be seen in the 'historization' of the myth through historiogenesis. The tone peculiar to the arguments of Clement, half comic, half embarassing, stems from this grossness of destruction" (OH, IV, 113). The lasting consequence of this dogmatic competition was that the rival historiographers familiarized themselves with one another's sources. Inadvertently this historiomachy created a history of the peoples of the Near East and Mediterranean basin that determined the Western understanding of world history until the late sixteenth century.

*

To follow Voegelin's argument further would be, strictly speaking, to move beyond the limits of the topic of historiogenesis to that of the genesis of world history. Nevertheless, a few further remarks may be useful in bringing to light some of the implications of the concept. First of all, ecumenical mankind, the contemporaneous population of the ecumene or the known world, may be distinguished from universal mankind. It is possible, at least in principle, to establish an ecumenic empire. In fact, according to Herodotus (VII: 8-11), that seemed to be the purpose of Xerxes's expedition against Hellas. At a preliminary strategy-session, Artabanus, Xerxes' uncle, persuaded him to call the invasion off by reminding him that "the God with his thunderbolt smites the overgrown creatures...He loves to bring low what rises too high." Then Herodotus told the story of how Xerxes had a dream that he would be deposed unless he continued the expedition. He was frightened by the experience and asked Artabanus to sleep in his bed, wearing his robes, and to see if he too had the dream. He slept, dreamt, and, as we know, the expedition went on to defeat. Herodotus's point, very simply, was that men are not persuaded by argument that the conquest of the ecumene is a sensible goal; they are moved by dreams when they sleep in the robes of kings. Where Xerxes failed, the Romans were a qualified success; and yet, Polybius' story of the victorious Scipio, weeping at the destruction of Carthage because of his foreboding that Rome would follow Carthage, as Carthage had followed Macedon, Persia, Media, Assyria, and Troy, showed that successful conquest was as limited in its meaning as

was defeat. Anaximander's <u>dictum</u> was eloquently expressed
in Scipio's tears.

A second problem arose with the success of the
ecumenical empires. As we saw, the earliest
historiogenetic speculations were bound to the particular
societies within which they developed. The resulting
conflicts in historiogenetic speculation, the
historiomachy just mentioned, perfectly expressed the
purposelessness of ecumenical conquest. Nevertheless,
it hid a more serious problem. The ecumene was not the
subject of an historiogenetic order, but a goal, a <u>telos</u>,
an object of conquest: "it was a graveyard of societies,
including those of the conquerors, rather than a society
in its own right" (<u>OH</u>, IV, 134). The question then
arose: to whom were these events happening? Who was
the subject of history? It was not any of the concrete
societies, since spiritually they were reduced to contestants in the historiomachy, and materially they were
merely constituent elements of the ecumenic organization.

According to Voegelin this problem of identity was
never completely thought through during the ecumenic
age of antiquity (<u>OH</u>, IV, 172). It was clear from Polybius
that the <u>telos</u> of ecumenical domination was inconclusive;
but in the Gospel of Matthew (24:12), "we find the missionary order which sounds like a deliberate literary answer
(though it hardly can be one) to Polybius: 'And this
gospel of the Kingdom shall be preached over the whole
ecumene, as a testimony to all nations; and then the
<u>telos</u> (the end, or fulfillment) shall come.'" The pragmatic
ecumene, thus, was no more than a prelude to the spreading

of the Gospel. Between the two men, Polybius and Matthew, was gained "the insight that the end of human action does not lie within this world but beyond it; this insight, which had been secured for personal existence by Plato in his Judgment of the Dead, has now expanded to include the telos of society in history. The fulfillment of mankind is an eschaton --the great theme of history and eschatology has opened."8 The "end" for Matthew, of course, was expressed in the apocalyptic symbolism of Daniel. Once again however, a new symbolism introduced a new problem: supposing that the ecumene were fully and successfully penetrated by the Gospel, what then? And what about those who died beforehand? An approximately successful solution to these questions was not found until St. Augustine's De Civitate Dei, an historiogenetic speculation, among other things, that brought a unilinear history to its meaningful telos in the dual ecumenism of the Church and the Roman Empire. The Church has since split into several denominations and the Empire into several states. Even at the time, the contemporaneous Sassanian Empire could have proved an obstacle to Roman ecumenism, and certainly since Voltaire's attack on Bossuet the whole structure had been in dispute.

Let us then return to Bossuet and Voltaire. The issue between them is suggested explicitly by the titles of their respective works.9 The former was burdened, under the heading of sacred history, with the unbearable weight of claiming to be the representative history of mankind, the historiogenesis of humanity. In fact, as Voltaire gleefully pointed out, it was no more than a parochial conflation of Israelite and Roman historiogenesis. His own attention to "the principal facts of history" had no trouble showing the defects of Bossuet's approach inasmuch as the parallel histories of China, Russia and the Muslim world were simply ignored. Bossuet, it seemed, had committed the same error as had the authors of the Sumerian King List. But what of Voltaire? He had, to his own satisfaction, replaced superstition with truth. Who, at least among his friends, would deny that the genuine history of humanity was an advance from barbarian rusticity to politeness?

A generation later, the experience of the French Revolution inspired several additional unilinear constructions, which have boiled down to such familiar orthodoxies as progressivism, Hegelianism and Marxism. At a purely factual level, these eighteenth- and nineteenth-century historiogenetic speculations have for some time been incompatible with the evidence for which they are pretended accounts.[10] One source of modern ideologies, therefore, and one factor that helps account for the persistence of ideologies in the face of contrary factual evidence may be sought in the experience, shared by modern ideologists and authors of the Sumerian King List, of the precariousness of social existence and the instability of historically contingent political forms. We have emphasized the common experience of anxiety as motivating equivalent efforts at tying a particular social or political order to an absolute starting point. The purpose of such efforts is to endow the presently existing order with ultimate significance.

Both Bossuet and Voltaire were arguing dogmatically. That is, they were operating with symbols as if they were concepts referring to the evidence of phenomena. Since the phenomena were evidently richer than Bossuet's frame of understanding would tolerate, Voltaire's argument appeared conclusive. To understand the whole question, however, one must also grasp the problematic status of the dogmatic form of the argument as well as its phenomenal content. Dogma, it was argued earlier, is a diminished and derived form of discourse. The origin of Bossuet's dogma was, of course, Christianity, whereas Voltaire's categories of meaning were anti-Christian dogmatic analogues (ER, 11). From analogue we are referred to dogmatic original and from there to its symbolic exemplar. In the case of Bossuet, for example, we would turn to Augustine and consider his civitas Dei and civitas terrena not as coextensive with ecclesiastical and secular organizations, co-partners in the sacrum imperium, but as expressions of an experience symbolized erotically by Augustine as the intentional objects of the two loves. In this way, one can apprehend an extension of potential "citizenship" in the heavenly city to all human beings, whether or not they have heard the Gospel or were members of medieval Christianitas.

Bossuet and Voltaire, however, each believed that their own partial historiogenetic myth in fact expressed the meaning of human universality. Voltaire was right to insist that the history of mankind could not be contained within an unreconstructed Augustinian framework, to say nothing of revived apocalyptic writings or of neo-Hellenic speculations. But Voltaire's own solution, even when

improved by Turgot and his successors during and after
the French Revolution, was hardly a tenable position,
whatever its popular success. The evidence for its theoretical inadequacy has, in fact, already been introduced:
countless individuals celebrate progress and technological wizardry in our society not for its own sake but
because it is understood as evidence that technological,
progressive society is the goal towards which all previous
historical actions have been straining. If we believe
the myth, the present inhabitants of the ecumene are
the privileged representatives of universal mankind simply
by virtue of their position on a unidimensional line of
time. But what to make of the interruption of this
chorus of self-congratulation by one such as George Grant?
What if, like Scipio at Carthage, he (or we) can find
no fulfillment in celebrating the dynamo? Either because
Grant is a philosopher, a spoudaios in Aristotle's sense,
or because his experience of the precariousness of the
present social order is understood by way of a different
historiogenetic symbolism, his objections invite us to
reconsider what the implications of the claim to universality mean. It should be clear that more is involved
than a personal problem of "religious commitment" or a
neurotic nostalgia. The issue engages the historian or
political scientist in their capacities as thinkers.

The question of historiogenetic universality, we
said, was much debated in the "historiomachy" of antiquity;
ideological polemics, hot and cold, with words or hardware,
serve the same purpose in the contemporary world. The
conclusion of the fictional conversation between Polybius
and Matthew was that the end or telos of human action

in the world lies outside the world, which is to say
that the end of society in history is an eschatalogical
question. According to Voegelin, the structure of the
question has not changed since antiquity, though its
terms have obviously been altered. Specifically, the
apocalyptic expectations of the "ecumene to come" (Heb.
2:5), which may make sense in an eschatalogical context,
cannot do so literally, within a historical context --to
prove this, all one needs do is consider the problems
involved in setting a date for the actual advent of the
new ecumene. If the argument so far be granted, it
follows that terms such as "universal humanity" or "universal mankind" must refer to a reality beyond that indicated
by historiogenetic myths, whether Sumerian, Augustinian,
or Voltairean.

This is hardly a violation of commonsense: if "mankind" (or an equivalent term) means anything, it means
the society of man in history, not the collection of
human beings who happen to be alive at the same time;
and the society of man in history, we know, extends
from an unknown beginning to an equally unknown end.
In Voegelin's words, terms such as "universal humanity"
indicate "man's consciousness of participating, in his
earthly existence, in the mystery of a reality that
moves towards its transfiguration. Universal mankind
is an eschatalogical index" OH, IV, 305). The meaning
of the symbols "universal mankind" or "universal humanity"
must be sought, therefore, in the consciousness of one's
own humanness and destiny; this universality can be
represented in living human beings only in their consciousness of the unknown beginning and end. Consequently,

it has nothing to do, experientially, with such
eighteenth-century notions as a "history of mankind"
where there is an implied story of a collectivity whose
climax of meaning issues in a present. One is referred
to such secondary symbols as Augustine's amor Dei or
Bergson's open soul to indicate a consciousness constitu-
tive of "history," where "history" is a symbol expressing
the experience of participation in the mystery of divine
presence.

Now, experience is always somebody's experience.
It would be wrong, therefore, to think that the experience
of "humanity" as the subject of "history" was a constant
feature of human consciousness. It may, in fact, be
lost more easily than it has been gained. At the very
least, Voegelin's analysis of historiogenesis will make
the identification of mankind with any political order,
ecumenical in its pretentions or not, the result of an
intellectual act of violent and narrow parochialism.
The motivation for these strange transformations of historically existing societies or power organizations into
a phenomenal subject of history, or the mythopoetic evoca-
tions such societies or power organizations in one's
imagination, as occurs in contemporary ideology, is found
in the anxiety that arises from a never quite suppressed
knowledge that what comes into existence, which includes
human beings both in their individuality and their plurality, will pass from existence. This awareness is equivalent
to the primary experience of the cosmos.

*

Some of the ways that Voegelin's concept might be used by historians and political scientists have been indicated en passant. These concluding summary comments are intended to do no more than recall three areas where the controversial aspects of Voegelin's work are most plainly evident.

First, there is Voegelin's habit of coining technical terms --historiogenesis, historiomachy, and so on-- when he finds the existing scholarly vocabulary deficient. In the past Voegelin has been accused of having invented a new jargon, and there is every reason to expect that the charge will be raised again regarding his later work. The only legitimate reply is that, from time to time, it is necessary to resort to neologisms to convey precisely and concisely an intended meaning. Of course, such terms may be abused and become not aids to thought but substitutes for it. For that, however, there seems to be no remedy. With respect to the concept dealt with in this chapter, it seems to me that the charge of jargon would be misapplied and that historiogenesis is in fact an unambiguous concept referring to a coherent configuration of phenomena and experiences that otherwise would remain, if not nameless, then partially identified by a series of less adequate terms.

A second objection that has been made of Voegelin's work may be repeated with respect to historiogenesis and, indeed, all the later volumes of Order and History. Critics have echoed G.S. Kirk's remarks about Levi-Strauss, that his methods are impervious to detailed verification unless "we can take all the material together in as much detail, and with as synoptic a vision, as he does." With Levi-Strauss, at least, the objection seems well taken: he seldom summarizes his argument but "ruthlessly continues a seemingly endless fugue of allusion."11 Voegelin, however, makes no claim to finality or system and, apart from the technical vocabulary he uses, presents no difficulties for specialists. Accordingly, there are no insuperable barriers arising from his broad interpretative strategy that would serve as effective means to prevent more focussed and specialized corrections of fact or emphasis. If there are conceptual, interpretative or factual errors they will be corrected soon enough by the community of scholars. There has been no abandonment of one of Voegelin's fundamental principles, that a comparative scholar must know what he is talking about.

The greatest difficulty, which has given rise to the most widespread and heated objections, concerns the broadest level of Voegelin's hermeneutics. Some of the problems have been touched upon already in the brief discussion in this chapter of Voegelin's understanding of "theory." We would conclude this discussion of historiogenesis with a recollection of the problem of interpretation in light of the questions we have just addressed.

Order and History began as an ambitious but more or less conventional study in philosophy of history, as we understand the term today. In the Introduction to Volume II, entitled "Mankind and History," for example, there was no discussion of the term as an eschatalogical symbol. Rather, Voegelin spoke of parallel streams of meaning intersecting with what he called "successive leaps in being," by which he meant the acts by which the structure of human experience is raised to consciousness. The insight derived from these acts consists, quite simply, in a new truth about human existence. For example, we saw above that the Biblical story of Adam and Eve expressed a truth concerning the imperfections of individuals more adequately than the story of the Adamites and their successors. In other words, the common human experience of imperfection can become more or less conscious, articulate, and explicit depending upon the insight, ability, and desire of a thinker who reflects upon it. Abstractly, at least, there is little to dispute with Voegelin's formulation. The real problems lie elsewhere.

Earlier in the course of Order and History, Voegelin remarked that a philosophy of history was not "an amiable record of memorabilia" governed by "the hope that the passions which have caused phenomena of the past to survive in the memory of mankind were judicious in their choice." On the contrary, it must be "a critical study of the authoritative structure in the history of mankind" namely, "the fact that the truth about the order of being emerges in the order of history. The Logos of history itself provides the instruments for the critical testing and ranking of the authoritative structure" (OH, II, 7). Voegelin's claim was unusual, but necessary to avoid two theoretical errors: on the one hand, historicist relativism, which abandoned any notion of an authoritative structure, and, on the other, pretense of declaring the meaning of history to be this or that, as is done with unfailing impudence by contemporary ideologists. Even when shored against these theoretical errors, however, history was still conceived "as a process of increasingly differentiated insight into the order of being in which man participates by his existence" (OH, IV, 1), and that is maximally differentiated in the discourse or authoritative judgement of the Aristotelian spoudaios or his equivalent. The means to discover this maximal differentiation was through the presentation of the principal types of symbolism and social order in historical succession. Again, this was an ambitious project, but one that clearly did not constitute a radical break with the conventions of philosophy of history.

With the introduction of the concept of historiogenesis, the very stability of historical succession as an order within which meanings appear became problematic. Now it was necessary to take account "of the important lines of meaning in history and that did not run along lines of time"; now "the analysis had to move backward and forward and sideways, in order to follow empirically the patterns of meaning as they reveal themselves in the self-interpretation of persons and societies in history" (OH, IV, 2, 57). Now, that is, the focus of the philosopher of history who in Voegelin's view was to be judged worthy of the name, must be on the constant features of human consciousness as they have been expressed through a series of historically variegated symbols.[12] Whether many philosophers of history, historians, political philosophers, or whatever will accept Voegelin's implicit (and sometimes not so implicit) challenge may be doubted, at least if the scholarly reception of the earlier volumes of <u>Order</u> <u>and</u> <u>History</u> serves as a guide. Nor does it seem likely that those whom one may call orthodox scholars in the disciplines just indicated will abandon their more specialized and technical studies to discuss with Voegelin broad and general questions of the meaning of human existence as it appears in its historical dimension.

Of course, nobody is obliged to read, let alone critically reflect upon, anybody's work. But it is not academic pluralism alone that leads one to anticipate scholarly silence. The reason for it seems to be that this area of Voegelin's work is the most difficult to come to terms with. When the focus shifts from an analytical consideration of texts or events to the theorist's claim that the insights expressed by way of the analyses constitute a new truth, then the very serious problems arise. Voegelin's concept of historiogenesis raises precisely this claim; accordingly, it contains the implicit demand of a specific experiential or existential (and not just scholarly or technical) commitment. Commenting upon an incident at a conference on comparative religion, where one participant raised the question as to whether "the science of comparative religion was an occupational therapy for persons otherwise unemployable, or whether it was a pursuit of the truth of existence which its subject-matter substantively contained," Voegelin remarked: "not everyone was pleased by such tactlessness."[13] When Voegelin raised equally indiscreet questions that, moreover, called into doubt the fundamental assumption of history, namely, the meaningfulness of historical succession, and when he replaced this apparently solid order of discourse with a theory of consciousness and the notion that lines of meaning may run sideways as well as backward and forward in time --when this happens, one may anticipate the response easily enough.

Yet, if Voegelin were rejected only because he is unorthodox, the result would be, at best, indecisive. He has, admittedly, introduced several large and demanding topics. Indeed, the very grandeur of his themes may serve to inhibit specialized criticism. However that may be, only a great thinker could raise such questions convincingly, and this alone should be sufficient motivation for historians, philosophers, and political scientists to get behind his words and recover the meanings they intend. In focussing upon the single concept, historiogenesis, we have tried to follow Voegelin's indications regarding the motivations for the creation of symbolisms in this form, the epistemology that spans the gap between personal experience and the public expression of it, and the criteria by which the symbolism and its engendering experience may be judged. In the following chapter we consider further Voegelin's theory of consciousness.

NOTES

[1] *Meaning in History: The Theological Implications of the Philosophy of History*, (Chicago, University of Chicago Press, 1949), 104.

[2] *Technology and Empire*, (Toronto, Anansi, 1969), 143.

[3] Voegelin, "Immortality: Experience and Symbol," 236.

[4] "Immortality," 248-249.

[5] Giorgio de Santilliana and Hertha von Dechend, *Hamlet's Mill: An Essay on Myth and The Frame of Time*, (London, Macmillan, 1969) esp. 56ff. and 323ff.

[6] See Seth Benardete, *Herodotean Inquiries*, (The Hague, Martinus Nijhoff, 1969), 131, 209; also Voegelin *OH*, II, 333 *et seq.*, and *OH*, IV, 105.

[7] Anaximander, B1: "From whatever is the coming-to-be of the things that are, into that will be their perishing (*phthora*) as a debt of necessity; for they pay the penalty and compensation to one another for their injustice according to the decree of time." Benardete, *op cit.*, 113 *et seq.*

[8] "World Empire and the Unity of Mankind," 184.

[9] Bossuet, *Discours sur l'Histoire Universelle* (1681): Voltaire, *Essai sur les Moeurs et l'Esprit des nations, et sur les principaux Faits de l'Histoire, depuis Charlemagne jusqu' à Louis XVIII* (1756).

[10] Archeological evidence from what Breasted termed the fertile crescent, which has been available since the mid-nineteenth century, led Eduard Meyer, early in this century in his *History of Antiquity*, to propose retaining the ancient-medieval-renaissance-modern unilinearity, but to apply it separately to distinct civilizational complexes. Thus, one could speak of

medieval Hellenic civilization, a Hellenic renais-
sance and so on. The tradition was continued with the
civilization parallels of Spengler and Toynbee. In
this rather recondite area of historiography,
Voegelin's part in the debate has been to argue in
effect, that the "civilizational units" employed, for
example, by Toynbee, were empirically inadequate.
Toynbee's universal states and universal religions
were not universal but ecumenic; nor were they the
end of civilizations (as Toynbee argued) but transi-
tional power-organizations that fragmented into ethnic
units similar to, but not identical with, the
pre-ecumenic societies. This vast configuration of
problems is the topic of The Ecumenic Age.

11
G.S. Kirk, Myth: Its Meaning and Functions in
Ancient and Other Cultures, (Cambridge, Cambridge
University Press, 1971), 59-60.

12
See below, Chapter Six, for a discussion of what these
"constant features" are.

13
Voegelin, "On Classical Studies," 6.

CHAPTER FIVE

COSMOS AND EMPIRE:
THE DIFFERENTIATION OF CONSCIOUSNESS

In a well known passage in The New Science of Politics, Voegelin wrote:

> Human society is not merely a fact, or an event, in the external world to be studied by an observer like a natural phenomenon. Though it has externality as one of its important components, it is as a whole a little world, a cosmion, illuminated with meaning from within by the human beings who continuously create and bear it as the mode and condition of their self-realization (NSP, 27).

The general equivalence of these political "externalities" is indicated by the familiar medieval functions, defence of the realm and administration of justice. No society can maintain its existence without defending itself against the outside and organizing itself internally. This, borrowing from Voegelin, may be called the elemental articulation of a society. "Elemental" does not mean unimportant. A society that neglects its arms, no matter how beautiful its laws, will soon wish it had attended to Machiavelli's teaching in the twelfth chapter of The Prince. Indeed, unilateral disarmament amounts to a prelude to social self-destruction. It takes little imagination to see that an absence of Machiavelli's "good arms" would entail not simply the destruction of the elemental externalities of a society, including its laws, whether they were good or not, but of the very pith and substance of social meaning. Indeed, the elemental externalities, the army, the police, the judiciary, the prisons, the bureaucrats who collect our taxes, the whole apparatus, in fact, of what we call our political institutions is in place to serve not its continued existence only, but an internal meaning, created and borne by the members of that society as "the mode and condition of their self-realization."

Voegelin's language in 1952 was not as precise as it became in his later work, but the sense of it is clear enough.[1] Any human society, in its aspect as an internal "cosmion," is meaningful. It is meaningful to its members because they participate in the "little world." Others who do not find it meaningful do not participate in it. Accordingly, they are not part of it. Perhaps they have their own "little world." In any event, the members of any given society who understand that they are indeed members of that society are members in virtue of their participation in its particular meaning. Moreover, they continuously create and maintain this meaning, which is what participation, in this context, is.

As for the cosmion itself, Voegelin used the imagery of vision and light to express its internal articulation. It is "illuminated," he said, with an elaborate symbolism. This symbolism, which varies from the comparatively unreflective immediacy of rite and ritual activity --dancing, for example-- through the mediation of language of myth and theory, "illuminates" insofar as it makes "the internal structure of such a cosmion, the relation between its members and groups of members, as well as its existence as a whole, transparent for the mystery of human existence." That is to say, the symbolism of the cosmion expresses the meaningful structure of a given society as an empirical order, in terms of something more meaningful still, which Voegelin here called the mystery of human existence. The symbols that illumine the cosmion make it "transparent" for another light, the mysterious light of existence itself.

We have, then, three "levels of reality" as Alfred Schutz called them: the level of elementary externalities, the empirical meanings that "illumine" these externalities, and the "mystery of human existence" for which the illuminating symbolisms are "transparent."[2] Together these levels of meaning constitute social reality, and they do so in a reciprocal fashion. The most immediate and massively empirical, the "elemental," is the least mysterious, whereas the "mystery of human existence" is expressed by mediation of the various symbolisms and therefore exists only by way of participation in its meaning. And yet, the mystery of human existence is a constant, whereas the elemental externalities are simply created by humans and also are destroyed by them. One may say, then, that the mystery of human existence being constant or, if you like, "eternal," is "more real" than the elemental externalities, which is to say that it is experienced by human beings as the source of meaning expressed in the symbolisms that order the cosmion that illumines

the elemental externalities. At the same time, this
eternal mystery exists only by the mediation of the
symbolisms. The symbolisms, then, are fully a mediation
between the massively existent, transient, and immediate
elemental externalities --the police and the tax
collector-- and the nonexistent, eternal, and mediated
"mystery of existence."

This summary exegesis of a few sentences of a small
book published a generation ago might lead an interpreter
into a consideration of any number of problems: What
is the relationship between the facts and events of the
external world and little world of meaning? Or between
it and that for which it is transparent? What is the
point of these images of light? How are they related
to prior imagery, to that of Plato, for example? How
are the elemental externalities recognized? What are
the dynamics of participation in the cosmion? What happens
when several cosmions meet? Are some of them more
meaningful? What would "more" mean in this case? What
exactly is this "mystery of existence" anyway? How is
it mediated by symbolisms? What does eternal or
nonexistent mystery mean, if anything? One could go
on.

The purpose of this chapter however, is more modest:
to draw together some of Voegelin's remarks on cosmos
and empire.[3] Now, empire is a term that, in the first
instance, refers to an elemental externality, an
institutional configuration of power and office.[4] Even
to commonsense, however, empires are distinguished not
simply in terms of their geographic extent, military

strength or internal organization. Nor are they distinguished merely by the dates of their existence. Certainly the human beings who live under imperial orders have insisted that their social life has a meaning. These meanings differ, as do the symbolisms that make the meanings articulate and apparent. One of the achievements of Voegelin's remarks on empire is that he has described the distinctive configurations of meaning that constitute the internal imperial world. In addition, of course, any particular inhabitant of an empire may, on occasion, experience the given symbolization of meaning as deficient in any one way or another. Such a one would describe the common meanings as error, evil, untruth, and so on. In these instances the given public symbolisms are not "transparent for the meaning of existence." On the contrary, they are "opaque." These occasions are precious, for they make visible the problematic relationship between the mystery of existence and political order as such. Accordingly, Voegelin has called them "differentiating" experiences.

In a conversation recorded in 1976 Voegelin distinguished four types of empire.[5] First, were imperialized ethnic societies identified in the first volume of Order and History as cosmological empires. Second were multicivilizational ecumenic empires studied in the fourth volume of Order and History. Third were the orthodox empires that emerged from the ecumenic empires, the Byzantine Eastern Orthodox, the Western Latin Orthodox, and the Islamic. These have never received an extensive and systematic analysis from Voegelin's hand though occasional remarks can be found in his essays and articles. We have summarized some of the aspects of his treatment of medieval western Christendom above in Chapter Two. The orthodox empires in turn disintegrated and were replaced by ideological empires. As with the orthodox empires, ideological empires have never been discussed under that particular head, though Voegelin has made several extensive analyses of ideological speculation and of ideological political action. In this chapter discussion is confined to the first imperial type only. To be precise, I shall consider but a handful of texts, chiefly from the Egyptian Dynasty XVIII. The symbolisms of the cosmological empires are first in chronological sequence. In addition, however, the specific modes of experience for which the cosmological symbolisms are transparent are first as well, in the sense of being what Voegelin called "primary."

*

There are, Voegelin wrote in the Introduction to Order and History, two basic forms of symbolization that characterize great periods in history. "The one is the symbolization of society and its order as an analogue of the cosmos and its order; the other is the symbolization of social order by analogy with the order of a human existence that is well attuned to being" (OH, I, 5). The imperial societies of the ancient near east were cosmological in the sense that political order was symbolized by cosmic analogies. Man and society were experienced as being ordered by the same elements of being that ordered the cosmos. Correspondingly, cosmic analogies "both express this knowledge and integrate social into cosmic order" (OH, I, 38). Seasonal vegetative and celestial rhythms constitute the overarching order that furnishes the analogies and makes them intelligible and persuasive.

The imperial cosmological societies were not, however, the earliest. "Practically all of the symbols that appear in the ancient Near East had a prehistory reaching through the Neolithicum back into the Paleolithicum, for a period of some twenty thousand years before the Near Eastern empires."[6] As a consequence of the discovery of new evidence regarding pre-imperial cosmological symbolism, new problems concerned with the defferentia specifica of imperial cosmological order have recently arisen.[7] Inevitably, there are also several polemical treatments that argue, in the teeth of archeological evidence, that predynastic Egypt was "Negro" and the perfection of "Negro" African civilization. These works, which have no scholarly or intellectual value, are nevertheless interesting documents for the study of the academic resentment that has followed the traumas of decolonization.

Considering only the imperial cosmological myths, Voegelin discussed three imperial "styles," the Chinese, the Mesopotamian and the Egyptian. A few comparative remarks were made in the first volume of Order and History about the Chinese style; many more concerned the Mesopotamian and Egyptian. Common to all three styles was the experience of founding a government, "an essay in world creation," and an analogical repetition of the divine creation of the cosmos. This act of creation made humans both partners and rivals of the gods or God. It brought cosmic responsibilities with it and induced anxieties on an equally grand scale, because, as was discussed in the preceeding chapter, the cosmos is not altogether stable. Men die; women and fields may be barren; cities fall to armies and earthquakes; eclipses occur and the equinoxes precess. Accordingly, rituals have been enacted on a periodic basis to retune the society with the cosmic rhythms and historiogenetic stories linked the political cosmion to the creation of the cosmos itself.

Perhaps as a consequence of a comparatively gradual change from village community through city state to empire, Mesopotamia managed to preserve an institutional, symbolic and experiential continuity, a "civilizational form," from around the fourth millennium until the foundation of the Achemenian Empire in the sixth century. This comparative rigidity and inflexibility is also apparent in a relative absence of what Voegelin called differentiating experiences.

Differentiated experiences of existence are historically distinct from the primary experience of the cosmos. As indicated earlier, the primary experience of the cosmos is structured according to the realities of God, man, world and society each of which participates in different degrees in an undifferentiated community of being (OH, I, 12-16). Differentiated experiences of existence do not consist in experiences of different reality but of the same reality in a distinct mode. In place of the overarching consubstantiality of the cosmos, the community of being is experienced as differentiated in terms of immanence and transcendence. This does not mean that the reality of existence in between immanence and transcendence is not there in "compact" (or nondifferentiated) experience. On the contrary, the tension of existence in-between is expressed, within the mode of primary cosmic experience, as one of hierarchy in lasting. That is, the symbolisms that express the primary experience of the cosmos are equivalent to the symbolisms that express the differentiated experiences indicated by the terms immanent and transcendent being. The difference between compact and differentiated experience lies in the degree of clarity with which the relationship of world-transcendent to intracosmic reality is made articulate.

In the first volume of Order and History Voegelin formulated three rules to describe the principles of compactness and differentiation of the experiences of order: "(1) The nature of man is constant. (2) The range of human experience is always present in the fulness of its dimensions. (3) The structure of the range varies from compactness to differentiation" (OH, I, 60). It is clear that the formula no less than the distinction between intracosmic and transcendent reality can be made only by a consciousness that experiences reality in the differentiated mode. This observation then raises the question: what moves consciousness from a compact to a differentiated mode? The answer, in principle, is simple: the "compact mode of symbolization will not do justice to structures of reality apprehended implictly but not

yet fully differentiated" (OH, IV, 75-6). The details
with respect to each spiritual outburst or "leap in
being" will vary according to a multitude of circumstances.
In this chapter we will consider one such spiritual
outburst, a partial differentiation or "leap in being"
that expressed an equally partial disintegration of the
imperial cosmological civilization form of Egypt.

As compared to Mesopotamia, the creation of the
Egyptian civilizational form was more rapid. There was,
of course, a cosmological experiential continuity with
tribal societies of the Levant and north-east Africa,
but the imperial institutional order was new. In this
respect, Pharaonic order, like the Mesopotamian, was
the continuous renewal and reenactment of the eternal
cosmic rhythms. Pharaoh mediated the divine substance,
maet, of the cosmos as god-king. Through him

> the god was manifest in society as a whole; and
> conversely, by being an Egyptian, the humblest
> peasant on his lands, or worker on his pyramid,
> participated in the divinity of the order that
> emanated from the Pharaoh; the divinity of the Pharaoh
> radiated over society and transformed it into a
> people of the god (OH, I, 74).

Efficient circulation of maet was ensured by Pharaoh's
bureaucrats. The imperial community, then, was held
together by maet, manifest in the world as a political
hierarchy. Any "differentiation" of experience would,
in the first instance, occur within the range of
consubstantiality, that is, of a partnership in being
flowing from divine to mundane and to human existences.

This was expressed most completely in the Memphite Theology, a body of texts that linked the One God, One Cosmos, and One Egypt into an impressive speculative construction and accounted for the establishment of Memphis as the new centre of a unified Egypt under Dynasty XXV in 712.

On the other hand, and rather more interesting, was the response to disorder. Three texts, all dating from around the troubled First Intermediate Period near the turn of the second millennium, show a remarkable range of response. In the "Song of the Harp-Player" the poet understood his present as no more than a link on the chain of generations; all that had been achieved by men was a collection of gods and beatified nobility lying in ruined pyramids.

> What are their places now?
> Their walls are broken apart, and their places are not--as though they had never been.

Not one of the dead has returned to tell of "the mystery of existence" and the material manifestations of eternity, the pyramids, had been looted. There was, Voegelin remarked "enough of an object lesson to awaken a sense of the gulf that separates the achievement of man from the eternity of being."[8] The harp-player's intellectual response, skepticism, was followed by an existential palliative, hedonistic indulgence:

> Follow thy desire as long as thou shalt live...
> Set an increase to thy good things;
> Let not thy heart flag.

Follow thy desire and thy good...
Make holiday, and weary not therein!
Behold, it is not given to any man to take his
property with him.
Behold, there is no one who departs who comes back
again!

A second text, of about the same period, is the
"Dispute of a Man, Who Contemplates Suicide, with his
Soul."[9] The text is divided into two parts. In the
first is found the dispute. The soul offered conventional
arguments against suicide: it was immoral and impious.
Man replied that exceptional circumstances justified his
violation of convention. Besides, Man promised to provide
for his Soul in the usual ritual way. To this the Soul
replied first with the harp-player's skepticism and then
suggested that hedonism was a way of forgetting the
cares of life, including suicide and what drove Man to
consider it. And Man replied: if he took such advice
his name would be a stench in the nostrils of men, like
bird-droppings, ripened fish, stagnant water, and other
unappetizing odors common to life on the banks of the
Nile even today. Man was alone in his existence, then,
without the conventional comfort of a conventional soul.

In the second part he described his loneliness:

To whom can I speak today?
One's fellows are evil;
The friends of today do not love...
To whom can I speak today?
There are no righteous;
The land is left to those who do wrong.

> To whom can I speak today?
> The sin that afflicts the land,
> It has no end.

In this condition, where the cosmic <u>maet</u> had disappeared, death was a deliverance to be welcomed, a release from years of captivity. The imagery is familiar to us as well from Greek and Biblical sources: life has become death. And the reversal turned death into the fullness of life. He who is yonder, in death:

> Will be a living god,
> Punishing the sin of him who commits it...
> Will stand in the barque of the sun,
> Causing the choicest therein to be given to the temples...
> Will be a man of wisdom
> Not hindered from appealing to Re when he speaks.

Suicide, then, was not a mere flight but rather a transfiguration and judgement. Man, in death, would be a companion and advisor of Re and a judge of human affairs. In the end the Soul agreed:

> Although thou be offered upon the brazier, still thou shalt cling to life, as thou sayest.

That is, even if Man died and was burned to a crisp, he would gain a new life.

In the "Dispute" the experience of consubstantiality was not abandoned though the institutional mediation of Pharaoh was. One may say, then, that the "civilizational form" had been cracked but not shattered. The Man of the "Dispute" had experienced enough of the mystery of existence to know that there was no hope for the institutionalization of maet along conventional lines: no new Pharaohs were in sight who could put things right. Accordingly, the Man offered himself as a substitute. In death Man would become a living god and a replacement for the ineffective and alive living god, Pharaoh, who had failed in his task. As a living god in death, Man hoped to be more effective than he was as a mere man existing in the living death of actual life. There was, however, no break with the cosmological symbolism: Man became a posthumous advisor to Re, not a prophet or philosopher. There was no transfer of authority from sacred kingship.

A third illustrative text is the "Prophecy of Nefer-rohu."[10] In this document the lector-priest Nefer-rohu spoke to Snefu, a Pharaoh of the Fourth Dynasty, and related the downfall of the Old Kingdom and the reestablishment of order under Amen-emhet I, the first Pharaoh of the Twelfth Dynasty. Nefer-rohu told of great natural and political disasters: the sun no longer shone, the river was empty of water, the winds opposed each other, the fish-ponds were damaged and the Asiatic armies were everywhere. "That which has never happened has happened." Murder went unpunished and sons killed their fathers; there were hordes of beggars and too many bureaucrats. "Re separates himself from mankind." Even the divine origin of maet had been destroyed: "The Heliopolitan nome, the birthplace of every god, will no (longer) be on earth." Accordingly, "Re must begin the foundation of the earth over again." On this foundation

Amen-emhet, the prophecy continued, will act: he will expel the Asiatics, unite Upper and Lower Egypt, silence the treacherous and restore the circulation of maet.

The literary form of prophecy dated from the Old Kingdom although the present text dates from the New, from the period of deliverance. Several aspects of this text are significant for the present topic. First, it is clear that the personal characteristics of the incumbent Pharaoh influenced the circulation of maet. Ritual mediation according to accepted formulae was not enough. But second, the author eliminated any mention of the previous rulers and the pragmatic course of prior history. The effect was to emphasize and heighten the symbolic expression of the direct divine-human encounter. In a time of disaster Re set the foundation in order again and Amen-emhet continued his divine work. Thirdly, the speculation on imperial order, as Voegelin said, "appears to be meant as a speculation on universal human order." For the author of the prophecy, that is, human status was closely tied to membership in the imperial society existing under divine dispensation. The enlargements of society from tribe to village, city, and empire were not simply quantitative increases in population but qualitative changes that decisively influenced the understanding of human beings. Political expansion and the foundation of the new political order were expressed concretely "as creative efforts by which man achieved a differentiated consciousness both of himself and of the divine origin of an order that is the same for all men" (OH, IV, 95). Reading history backwards from the restored imperial present of the author, one arrived at the divine foundation act by Re; reading it forwards from the divine dispensation, one arrived at the author's messianic present. On the occasion of imperial disintegration and restoration, the empire became transparent for the representation of humanity, but the humanity so represented evidently did not include the Asiatics or the treacherous.

A further loosening of imperial exclusiveness, though hardly a break in the civilizational form, is found in what is conventionally called the Amarna age.[11] The events centre on the activities and writings associated with Akhenaten (1373-57) though there is still considerable disagreement about what he did or did not do and even more on the significance to be accorded his actions. Nevertheless, Voegelin is certainly correct to remark that his activity had antecedents and causes,

> and an appraisal of its precise nature requires an understanding of the circumstances that would, for a few years, open the historical clearing in which he could move, only to close in again and cut his work short with abrupt failure (OH, I, 101-2).

In particular, the vicissitudes of the Pharaonic order prior to the rule of Dynasty XVIII, established after the expulsion of the Hyksos, meant a diminution of the prestige of Pharaoh and a corresponding increase in the prestige of the priests who served the longer lasting regime of the gods. Of these, the priesthood of Amun, at Thebes, was especially important.

The oracles of Amun initially had induced Ahmose to fight the Hyksos. His son, Amenophis I (1550-28), founder of Dynasty XVIII, carried the war south into Nubia; his successor Tuthmose I (1528-12) consolidated the southern frontier and drove through Syria to the Euphrates, where his soldiers were astonished to find a river that flowed the wrong way, north to south.[12] Tuthmose I was, as Redford pointed out, no traditionalist. He moved the capital south from Heliopolis to Memphis; he began work at Thebes to transform a provincial shrine of Amun into a giant state temple; he had his tomb excavated in the lonely wady known today as Biban el-Muluk, the Valley of the Kings; he separated his tomb from his mortuary chapel, which signalled the final abandonment of the pyramid form.[13]

Further innovation followed. The de facto rule of Hatshepsut was itself a novelty; she courted the Amun cult in order to increase her legitimacy, which also had the effect of raising the status of Amun's priests. Her memorial temple on the west bank at Thebes and not far from the Valley of the Kings was an architectural novelty.[14] Her nephew, Thutmose III (1503-1450), pursued a successful and ruthless military career the proceeds of which helped finance the Amun temple at Karnak. Upon her death (ca. 1482) he became sole king and systematically effaced her name from public monuments. This was not so much an act of personal vendetta as of political shrewdness: it served to link the new king with Thutmose I and add to his legitimacy. And, in any event, he left the queen's cartouche and figure intact when they were out of the public eye, in the sanctum of a shrine, for example.

The successful Asiatic wars were victories for Amun; Hatshepsut's courting of the Amun cult increased the political visibility of the priesthood. The first prophet, Hapuseneb, for example, bore the titles "overseer" and "great chief" of Upper Egypt in addition to his prophetic ones. "The situation," Redford remarked, "contained a conflict in embryo: two divine giants could not both share the spotlight....Just where, in actual fact, did the right to govern lie, with Amun or with the king?"[15] Likewise Voegelin discerned a "latent tension" in the account given by Thutmose III of his own divine nomination.[16] On the one hand, Thutmose recorded the victories he had won --for Amun, to be sure, but "through the work of my hands." On the other, he described them as discharging a debt: "I repay his good with good greater than it." Sooner or later the debt would be paid in full.

For three generations Egypt was comparatively peaceful and exceedingly prosperous. Akhenaten's father, Amenophis III (1402-1365), for example, was able to conduct foreign policy on the basis not of conquest and war but by diplomacy and lavish bribery. Through conquest Egypt had become a great empire; judicious administration and disorganized enemies had enabled it to rule the territory from Nubia to the Euphrates. During the time of Akhenaten (1373-57) the latent universalism of the empire found a new expression.[17] The stage for his performance had, however, been set by earlier generations.

Akhenaten's innovations were both institutional and spiritual. The institutional changes were straightforward: just as Amun had gained a large temple, a "horizon," or an "origin" or "resting-place," (ahket) during the time of Thutmose I, so Akhenaten provided one for the Aten. At Thebes the Aten was always just a visitor; he could hardly have evicted Amun, no more than he could have expelled Ptah from Memphis or Re-Atum from Heliopolis. So Akhenaten built him his own "horizon." The evidence that Akhenaten picked a fight with the Amun priests at Thebes because they were constituting an imperium in imperio or that he withdrew to Akhet-Aten in resentment and carried on a persecution of Amun from there is nonexistent. As Aldred observed, such an interpretation "was an invention of nineteenth-century historians, obsessed by contemporary struggles between Church and State in Europe."[18] Inevitably, the Amun Shrines would have been neglected, but there is no reason to assume that the priests would not be employed at the Aten ones. Certainly it is true that the great temple at Karnak continued to function even after the Amarna site was in operation.[19]

The spiritual changes were significant, though they were not innovations from whole cloth either. The prehistory of the Aten, Voegelin remarked, was obscure, though it is not perhaps as obscure today as it was a generation ago. The word Aten appears in the Middle Kingdom story of Sinuhet where the king's passing is described as follows:

The god entered his horizon (ahket),

The King of Upper and Lower Egypt,
Sehetep-ib-Re departed into the sky,
Uniting himself with the Aten.
The divine members became blended with
him who created them.[20]

A similar description was given the death of Amenophis
I:

He ascended to the sky, he united himself to the
Aten,
He became blended with him out of whom he had come.[21]

Thutmose I bore the title "Horus-Re, Mighty Bull, beloved
by Truth, with sharp horns, who comes out of the Aten."[22]
And, as Voegelin remarked, there is a hymn from the
reign of Amenophis III, "Praise to Amon, when he rises
as Horus of the Horizon." In this hymn the sun is
praised as Re and Khepri and then as "the Aten of Re of
the day," again as Horus, and as "the fashioner and
builder of that which the soil produces, the Khnum and
Amon of mankind." Finally the god is identified as a
world-god shining not only over the two lands of Egypt,
but

the sole lord, who reaches the ends of all lands
every day, being (thus) one who sees them that
tread thereon....Every land is in rejoicing at his
rising every day, in order to praise him.[23]

In all these texts, the emphatic attribute of the Aten
is that it is the visible origin or creative ground
from which the king first and later, mankind, emerges

and to which they return. The invisible origin, accordingly, is Amon. Voegelin remarked that during the period prior to Akhenaten the search for the nature of divine being was sufficiently underway that "a new name had to be found, in order to characterize its oneness and supremacy as lying beyond the Egyptian pantheon" (OH, I, 108). The novelty is, perhaps, overemphasized, though the style given to the relation of Aten to Amon by Akhenaten was innovative.

In the famous "Hymn to Amon-Re," which dates from a period prior to the reign of Akhenaten, it was Amon who was identified as a universal creator and sustainer of life:

> Thou art the sole one, who made all that is,
> The solitary sole one, who made what exists,
> From whose eyes mankind came forth,
> And upon whose mouth the gods came into being...
> Solitary sole one, with many hands,
> Who spends the night wakeful, while all men are asleep,
> Seeking benefit for his creatures.

A few years later the Aten was identified in a language that Breasted, among others, compared to Psalm 104.[25] Many of the sentiments indirectly expressed earlier were now made explicit:

> Thou appearest beautifully on the horizon of heaven,
> Thou living Aten, the beginning of life.
> When thou art risen on the Eastern Horizon
> Thou hast filled every land with thy beauty.

The Aten banished darkness and awakened Egypt to praise;
the beasts were content and the plants flourished, the
ships were kept safe, the women were fertile and the
men fecund, all thanks to the Aten.

> O sole god, like whom there is no other!
> Thou didst create the world according to thy desire
> Whilst thou wert alone...
> The countries of Syria and Nubia, the land of Egypt,
> Thou settest every man in his place,
> Thou suppliest their necessities:
> Everyone has his food, and his time of life is
> reckoned.
> Their tongues are separate in speech
> And their natures as well;
> Their skins are distinguished
> As thou distinguishest the foreign people.

Just as the Aten had made the Egyptian Nile to sustain
the people of the Two Lands, so he set a Nile in heaven
(that is, rain) for the benefit of the foreign people.

> For thou art the Aten of the day over the whole
> earth.

The Aten had become the creator god of mankind and sustainer
of all men, including the foreigners. "Their common
humanity," Voegelin wrote, "becomes apparent in spite
of their racial, linguistic and cultural differences.
The god is now understood as a god for all men" (OH, I,
108). Even so, the "Hymn to the Aten" was not monotheist
(Re, Horus, and Shu are also mentioned), nor did it
proclaim a universal redeemer-god.

On the contrary. The attribution of heavenly pharaonic attributes to the Aten, such as his acquisition of a titulary and of names incorporated in two cartouches, or the joint jubilee celebration of the Aten and of Akhenaten in year 12, or the correspondence of his regnal years with Akhenaten, had the complementary consequence of divinizing more emphatically Akhenaten.[26] It is his harking back to the divinity of Pharaoh characteristic of the Old Kingdom that allowed Voegelin and Aldred both to call his move "reactionary." Indeed, his change of nomen from Amenophis IV to Akhenaten carried the weak meaning "Servicable to the Aten" but also the much stronger one "The Effective Spirit (=incarnation) of the Aten."[27] The implication of his name, by this second reading, was that the meaning manifest in the solar orb was identical with that manifest in the flesh of the King. Ever since the days of Thutmose III the notion of "one god, one king" had been emphasized. Akhenaten drew the consequence that he alone was the mediator.

> Thou art in my heart,
> And there is no other that knows thee
> Save thy son Akhenaten
> For thou hast made him well-versed in thy plans
> and in thy strength.[28]

Funerary prayers were no longer addressed directly to the gods. On the Amarna coffins they all went via Akhenaten who in turn dealt only with the Aten, virtually ignoring the other divinities.[29]

As mentioned earlier, Voegelin remarked that the deeds and words of Akhenaten formed a complex structure,

both revolutionary and reactionary (OH, I, 105). Aldred
essentially agreed. Piankoff summarized the movement
as follows: "Amarna did not proclaim a new religion;
the ideas it sponsored came from the old stock....From
the purely religious point of view it was, like so many
controversies, a question of nuance, of a dogmatic
finesse."[30] There were several new emphases and a novel
representative symbolism,[31] but there was no break in
civilizational form. "To be sure," Voegelin concluded,
"the king was an extraordinary individual. Nevertheless,
when all is taken into account, his work reveals the
impasse of the Pharaonic symbolism rather than a new
beginning. He was a mystical aesthete of high rank and
could animate the form, for the last time, with his
spiritual fervor. But that was all, as far as the political
order of Egypt was concerned" (OH, I, 110). For one
reason or another, Akhenaten failed to deal with the
unrest on Egypt's northern borders; by the year 12 of
his reign, Egypt had lost its Asiatic empire. The
chronology of the end of Dynasty XVIII is still confused:
what is clear is that Tutankhamen (1357-49) who succeeded
as Tutankhaten, returned to many of the old religious
forms. Tutankhamen's successor Ay (1349-46) was shortly
replaced by his general, Haremhab (1346-15) who revised
the king-lists to make himself the direct successor of
Amenophis III. The Rameseside kings of Dynasty XIX
systematically villified those of Dynasty XVIII,
especially Akhenaten. This was not, in itself, unusual.
It did, however, reinforce the civilizational form, which
"remained unshaken to the end by foreign conquest" (OH,
I, 110).

*

Voegelin began Order and History with the famous
prefatory statement: "The order of history emerges from
the history of order." This may be taken as a summary
restatement of the opening remark of The New Science of
Politics: "The existence of man in political society
is historical existence; and a theory of politics, if
it penetrates to principles, must at the same time be a
theory of history." A third restatement was made in
the opening of Anamnesis: "The problems of human order
in society and history originate in (entspringen) the
order of consciousness. For this reason, philosophy of
consciousness is the chief component (Kernstuck) of a
philosophy of politics." These sentences do not conflict,
though the emphases are different. In particular,
Voegelin's work following the publication of the third
volume of Order and History has centered upon the process
of consciousness as it appears through its variegated
historical forms. So far as the Egyptian materials are
concerned, the following historical point has been
established: the Egypt of Dynasty XVIII was a political
order that, for the space of a century or so, gained
the elemental articulation of a great empire. Thanks
to good arms it carried its law far beyond the narrow
green valley of the Nile. The several hymns and texts
just considered expressed and explored the implications
of the meaning of the empire as a unit ruled by a single
king who was the mediator of, and advocate before, a
god who was somehow not like the others. In the fourth
volume of Order and History Voegelin discussed a few
pertinent aspects of this sort of consciousness.

As indicated above, the mode of consciousness expressed in the Egyptian texts Voegelin called "the primary experience of the cosmos." This cosmos is neither the physical universe nor the world created by a world-transcendent god. It is the whole: the gods, the celestial bodies, the terrestrial bodies and the movements of the entire company. This community of being, to use our earlier language, is experienced as consubstantial rather than differentiated. Kings act by divine mandate; the triumphs and defeats of the kingdom are a consequence of divine dispensation. It is precisely this structural connection between divine-cosmic and mundane-cosmic events that makes any interpretation of the Akhenaten interlude that posits conflict between a resentful king and a truculent caste of Amun priests at Thebes so anachronistic. As Aldred remarked, "when a god governed the land, his wishes and decrees were taken as inspired; and whether they were wise, criminal, beneficent or stupid could only be seen in retrospect when the god had ceased to rule."[32] At the same time, however, there was always the knowledge that the god might cease to rule, that the king might be unable to mediate the divine maet properly, that the cosmic divinity might diminish or go away. In the Aten hymn quoted earlier, it may happen that, in the countries of Syria, Nubia, and the land of Egypt, men forget their place or that necessities are not supplied. Perhaps even the common humanity of the foreigners, which once appeared through the shining of the Aten on all people, would be eclipsed. "On such occasions," Voegelin observed, "the cosmological style becomes transparent for a truth about God and history beyond the truth of the cosmos. In

spite of its embracingness, the shelter of the cosmos
is not safe --and perhaps it is no shelter at all" (OH,
IV, 70). What then? Where is shelter to be found? If
the gods are as much a part of the cosmos as the imperial
power organization, would not a political disaster arouse
apprehensions about a twilight of the gods?

The answer we know from the "Song of the Harp-Player"
and the "Dispute of a Man ... with his Soul." Skepticism
and anxiety about the cosmos and its order did occur.
And yet there was no break. Indeed, if the chronology
of the Akhenaten interlude is reliable, the king's
insistence upon his singularity as mediator was
contemporary with the disintegration of the northern
marches of the empire. That is, the despair and anxieties
aroused by political disorder can do no more than make
people receptive to a new style of truth and meaning.
Of themselves, therefore, such troubling moods are but
miseries to be endured.

A new truth appears, persuades, and gains acceptance
through the process Voegelin called differentiation. A
differentiated symbolization provides an understanding
of reality that is more adequate than existing
comparatively compact insights. In order to be understood
as more adequate, the differentiated symbolization is
grasped as a truer "account" of the same reality. From
the Egyptian materials it is apparent that this primary
experience is one of mutually reinforcing and intracosmic
analogies: the Aten is the god, Akhenaten is his
incarnation, etc. The validity or, if you like, the
acceptability, of the analogies depends upon a prior,

inarticulate, ante-predicative experience of an embracingness that provides coherence to the analogy, but is not of itself an element in it. In Voegelin's words,

> the cosmos is not a thing among others; it is the background of reality against which all existent things exist; it has reality in the mode of nonexistence. Hence, the cosmological play with mutual analogies cannot come to rest on a firm basis outside itself; it can do no more than make a particular area of reality (in this case: society and its order in history) transparent for the mystery of existence over the abyss of nonexistence (OH, IV, 72).

There is nothing outside of itself because there is nothing outside of reality. And in that "nothing" as the "outside" of reality lies the experience of a common ground, namely, the emergence of existence from nonexistence, and its precarious continuation on the edge of nonexistence. The peculiarity of cosmological analogies is that this common ground, on the basis of which all new truths arise as a differentiated challenge, is the "own ground" of the primary experience. That is, the experience of the cosmos is the experience of a balance or tension between existence and nonexistence, of emergence from "nothing" and a return to "nothing."

In light of the foregoing, we may recall an earlier remark, that the disintegration of the compact cosmological style of truth in favour of more differentiated symbolization is a consequence of the

comparative inability of the cosmological style to express
a more differentiated reality experienced. Specifically,
the means of symbolization, namely intracosmic, mutually
reinforcing analogy, does not adequately articulate the
balance or tension between existence and nonexistence.
Why not? Because everything, all reality, is symbolized
as an order of intracosmic things: the intracosmic
existing things --the Nile, the birds and frogs, the
Empire-- are consubstantial partners in the divine cosmos;
the nonexisting cosmos or the divine ground out of which,
or for which, the existing things exist, is symbolized
as the intracosmic gods --Amun, Re, Horus of the Horizon,
and eventually the sole one, the Aten. The problem is
that the presupposition of consubstantiality, which is
necessary if the analogies are to make sense, is
contradicted by the experience of hierarchy --of lasting
and passing, for example. Some of the "things" are
apparently more "cosmic" than others. Thus, the universe
and the gods assume the higher cosmic functions of the
nonexistent divine ground. Unfortunately, the universe
turns out to be far too existent to serve this purpose,
just as the gods are experienced as too nonexistent to
be intracosmic things. In Voegelin's words, "the tension
of reality has been absorbed into the wholeness of the
intermediate reality that we call cosmic and encloses
in its compactness the tension of existence toward the
ground of existence. Hence the cosmos is tensionally
closed"(OH, IV, 77). The tensional closure, then, is
what erodes and finally dissolves the cosmological
symbolism because it is experienced as untrue: the world
is not full of gods; the gods are not in the world.
Thus does the cosmological style of truth crack into a

dissociated and experientially differentiated pair, a dedivinized external world and a world-transcendent divinity. In conceptual language, the openness of the soul entails that a tensionally closed cosmos will be experienced as being inadequately symbolized by cosmic analogies. That is, cosmic analogies of the whole will be experienced as "untrue" or "the lie."

*

Only from the perspective of a differentiated consciousness does the problem of empire and cosmos appear in its constituent elements. The symbolization of political order by means of cosmic analogies is distinct from imperial power organization; moreover, a cosmological empire, despite its size, suffers no obligation to subject contiguous peoples to its rule nor to bring great swaths of real estate under its sway. Finally, the coexistence of several cosmological empires is not experienced as an unbearable contradiction, no more so, in fact, than is the coexistence of several cosmological tribes. When, furthermore, a cosmological empire undertakes a policy of expansion, there is no necessary implication that it is seeking to become an ecumenic empire. In the case of Thutmose III, for example, his military career probably had as much to do with the ambitions of his coregent, Hatshepsut. No doubt she was as pleased with Thutmose's victories as she was with the fact that his winning of them kept him abroad much of the time.

Nevertheless, when the empire did expand beyond the ethnic area of its origin, cracks and strains appeared in the cosmic analogue. The Amun Hymns and the Hymn to the Aten show an unmistakable tendency to differentiate the unknown divinity beyond or behind the familiar ennead. Likewise there appeared in outline the notion of a "mankind." This "mankind" was not, however, a truly universal mankind embracing all human beings, past, present and future, and all living under a divine dispensation. The movement, rather, was in the direction of political literalism.

The dynamics of this process may be summarized briefly. The military victories of Thutmose III, one may say, were the preconditions for the material prosperity and speculative exuberance of his successors. But a short century later Amenophis III presided over the next to inevitable disintegration of power that follows when money replaces arms as the effective means of conducting foreign policy. And his successor, Akhenaten, neglected the practice of arms almost entirely. His internal administration was also inept. A beautiful soul might be tempted to applaud his otherworldliness; but this is, rather, a romantic indulgence for which there is no evidence. In any case, even if Akhenaten were as accomplished a general as Thutmose III, it does seem clear that any attempt to represent the implicit or inarticulate universalism of the Amarna age by way of an imperial political organization would encounter in direct form the contradictions indicated earlier. Akhenaten's "reactionary" streak in proclaiming himself sole mediator between mankind (or at least that fragment of it under his rule) and the sole divinity, the Aten, expressed the contradiction in the form of political literalism.

Other instances of cosmic-imperial literalism are not difficult to imagine. The analogic rule over the four quarters of the world, for instance, could have become a literal rule over a territory whose limits were set only by opposing power. The analogic rule, however, took its meaning not from territorial domination but from the revolution of the celestial bodies that determined the four quarters. The "derailment" as Voegelin called such literalism, appears to be inherent in the process of symbolization and a constant factor in aggressive political expansion ever since the third millennium.

Only with the Israelite Moses and the Chosen People does one find an example of differentiated consciousness prior to the age of ecumenic empires. In the tribes he led from bondage in Egypt Moses found a pragmatic ethnic carrier for his spiritual movement. The new form of society was not focussed on imperial power but upon an exodus from it. As a consequence, Israel became a people under the kingship of a world-transcendent divinity which did not, however, exempt them as a people exposed to the vicissitudes of pragmatic power. The spiritual exodus from the compactness of the cosmological form was useless without the pragmatic power to defend the ethnic group that undertook it. But the creation of such a power seemed to entail a restoration of something like the cosmological institutions from which the pragmatic exodus was undertaken. The historical existence of Israel on the fringes of Egyptian imperial power and later at the crossroads of several other imperial powers struggling to dominate the world sustained a new but equivalent symbolization; it existed, however, only against the background of the cosmological form, transparent for the mystery of existence experienced as, and expressed by, the complex, cosmos and empire.

NOTES

[1] A study of the changes in Voegelin's language would be a rewarding enterprise, particularly as he has become increasingly aware of the importance of language symbols as expressions of reality experienced. In his later work, for example, one would never find a term such as "self-realization." Ellis Sandoz remarked correctly: "Recovery of the language of science is a major dimension of Voegelin's entire work from the 1930s onward." The Voegelinian Revolution: A Biographical Introduction (Baton Rouge: Louisiana State University Press, 1981), 15.

[2] See in particular Schutz, "Symbol, Reality, and Society," in Maurice Natanson, ed., Collected Papers, vol. I, The Problem of Social Reality (The Hague: Martinus Nijhoff 1962), part III, 205 et seq., and Helmut R. Wagner, "Agreement in Discord: Alfred Schutz and Eric Voegelin in Peter J. Opitz and Gregor Sebba, eds., The Philosophy of Order: Essays on History, Consciousness and Politics for Eric Voegelin on his Eightieth Birthday (Stuttgart: Klett-Cotta, 1981), 74 et seq.

[3] Not all power organizations are empires. There exist pre-imperial neolithic civilizations often in an indeterminate quasi-tribal form, the Greek polis, monastic political organizations, and the national state, to list only the most obvious. Some of these social configurations could be discussed under the category of civilization. Even so, as Geoffrey Barraclough remarked: "The theme of empire looms large in Eric Voegelin's writing." Eric Voegelin and the Theory of Imperialism," in Optiz and Sebba, eds., The Philosophy of Order, 173.

[4] The English word empire is derived from the Latin imperium, which conveyed the general meaning of power and command and denoted specifically the legal power of command. Throughout its career, however, the term

has also meant greatness and renown. For this reason it is not misleading to speak of an Athenian empire or of the empire of Rameses II though the term does not appear in the sense we mean before the time of Scipio Africanus. For details, see the survey of Richard Koebner, _Empire_ (Cambridge: Cambridge University Press 1961).

5
Conversations with Eric Voegelin, ed., R. Eric O'Connor (Montreal: Thomas More Institute Papers, 1980), 117.

6
Voegelin "Autobiographical Memoir."

7
For details on the several predynastic societies of the Nile Valley. See Elise J. Naumgartel, "Predynastic Egypt, "_Cambridge Ancient History_, 3rd ed., (Cambridge: Cambridge University Press, 1970), I: 1, 463-97, H. Alimen, _The Prehistory of Africa_, tr. A.H. Brodrick, (London: Hutchinson, 1957), ch. 3, or A.J. Arkell, _The Prehistory of the Nile Valley_, (Leiden: Brill, 1975). I.E.S. Edwards, "The Early Dynastic Period in Egypt," _Cambridge Ancient History_, I: 2, 1-70 is also useful as are Cyril Aldred, _Egypt to the End of the Old Kingdom_, (London: Thames and Hudson, 1965), and Walter B. Emery, _Archaic Egypt_ (Baltimore: Penguin, 1961).

8
OH, I, 59. The text of the song is taken from John A. Wilson's translation in James B. Pritchard, ed., _Ancient Near Eastern Texts Relating to the Old Testament_ (Princeton, Princeton University Press, 1950), 467. Subsequent references are to A.N.E.T. A variant is found in James H. Breasted, _The Dawn of Conscience_, (New York: Scribners, 1953), 163 ff. See also Wilson's discussion in _The Culture of Ancient Egypt_, (Chicago, University of Chicago Press, 1951, 113 ff.

9
Translation by Wilson in Pritchard, ed., _A.N.E.T._, 405-07. See also Breasted, _The Dawn of Conscience_,

168-78; Voegelin's analysis in <u>OH</u>, I, 98 ff should be supplemented by his later remarks in "Immortality: Experience and Symbol," 241-48.

10
Translation by Wilson in Pritchard, ed., <u>A.N.E.T.</u>, 44 f. Voegelin's analysis is in <u>OH</u>, I, 1-4 ff and <u>OH</u>, IV, 91 ff. Breasted's version is in <u>The</u> <u>Dawn</u> of Conscience, 201 ff.

11
The title is anachronistic, being derived from the modern site, Tell el-'Amarna; it was first excavated by a French mission during 1883-1893. The ancient name was Akhet-Aten, The Horizon (or Resting-Place) of the Aten. Voegelin's account in <u>Order</u> <u>and</u> <u>History</u> I, 101 ff., relies largely on Wilson and Breasted and needs to be supplemented with later analyses by Aldred, Anthes, Piankoff, Giles, and Redford. Reports of the year's work at Amarna are regularly published in the <u>Journal</u> <u>of</u> <u>Egyptian</u> <u>Archeology</u>. A useful summary of a recent dig at Karnak and Luxor is Donald B. Redford, "The Razed Temple of Akhenaten," <u>Scientific</u> <u>American</u>, 239 (Dec. 1978), 136-47. The older treatment by Breasted in the first edition of <u>The</u> <u>Cambridge</u> <u>Ancient</u> <u>History</u> has been brought up to date in William C. Hayes, "Egypt: Internal Affairs from Tuthmosis I to the Death of Amenophis III," in <u>Cambridge</u> <u>Ancient</u> <u>History</u>, 3rd ed., (Cambridge, Cambridge University Press 1973), II:1, 313-415 and Cyril Aldred, "Egypt: The Amarna Period and the End of the Eighteenth Dynasty," in <u>ibid</u>., II:2, 49-96. The work of Cerny and Gardiner is also very useful regarding details.

12
In fact the Egyptian word for the Euphrates was "inverted water."

13
Donald B. Redford, <u>History</u> <u>and</u> <u>Chronology</u> <u>of</u> <u>the</u> <u>Eighteenth</u> <u>Dynasty</u> <u>of</u> <u>Egypt</u>, (Toronto: University of Toronto Press, 1967), 79.

14
It is presently being restored by a Polish archeological mission. From a distance it looks Greek.

[15] History and Chronology, 84.

[16] OH, I, 104-5. The text, "The Divine Nomination of Thutmose III" is from the wall of the Amun temple at Karnak and is translated in Pritchard, ed., A.N.E.T., 446-7.

[17] The regnal dates of Amenophis III and Akhenaten overlap because they were coregents.

[18] Syril Aldred, Akhenaten: Pharaoh of Egypt--A New Study, (London: Thames and Hudson, 1968), 193. The only evidence at all is from Tut-ankh-Amun's Restoration Stella, which reports that he could not find a cadre of priests to resume office in the newly re-opened shrines. There is no evidence of a "theological" antagonism. A translation of the text is in Adolf Erman, "Geschichtliche Inschriften aus dem Berliner Muzeum," Zeitschrift fuer aegyptische Sprache und Altertumskunde, 38 (1900), 112.

[19] Voegelin's account, OH, I, 105-6, relied chiefly on Meyer (1962), Wilson (1951) and Breasted (1933) and must be considered dated with respect to details of the political activities of Ahkenaten.

[20] J.H. Breasted, ed. and tr., Ancient Records of Egypt (Chicago, University of Chicago Press, 1970), Ancient Records, Series 2, Vol. I, 486 ff. Sehetep-ib-Re is the praenomen of Amenemhet I, first king of Dynasty XII.

[21] Tr. Sethe (1914) quoted in Alexandre Piankoff, tr., N. Rambova, ed., The Shrines of Tut-Ankh-Amon (New York, Bollingen, 1955), 6.

[22] Tr. Gautheir (1917) quoted in Piankoff, op. cit., 6.

[23] OH I, 106: the text if in Pritchard, ed., A.N.E.T. 367-8 and in Breasted, Dawn of Conscience, 276. The phrase "Khnum and Amon of mankind" carried a pun; khnum, is builder, amon is hidden. Thus the Aten is Horus etc. and the hidden builder of mankind.

[24] Text in Pritchard, ed., A.N.E.T., 366.

[25] Breasted, The Dawn of Conscience, 281 ff. Text is in Pritchard, ed., A.N.E.T., 369-71.

[26] For details see Aldred, Akhenaten, 168 ff, and his article "The Beginning of the El-'Amarna Period," Journal of Egyptian Archeology, 45 (1959), 19-33.

[27] Aldred, Akhenaten, 185.

[28] Pritchard, A.N.E.T., 371.

[29] Aldred, Akhenaten, 191. For typical texts, see Breasted, Ancient Records, II, 1000-1013.

[30] Piankoff, The Shrines of Tut-Ankh-Amon, 12-13.

[31] The most interesting symbolic innovation, apart from enclosing the name of the Aten in two royal cartouches, was the introduction of the visible representation of a disk from which diverging beams radiated downwards each ending in a human hand, some of them bringing the ankh of life to the nostrils of King and Queen (and to them alone). The new depiction carries the old meaning of a "many-handed" god (for example, in the "Hymn to Amun-Re," A.N.E.T., 366) and of exclusive royal mediation. In addition, the degree of abstraction suggests universality much more easily than anthropomorphic, theriomorphic, or zoomorphic gods. A good number of years ago Sir E.A. Wallis Budge drew attention to the similarity of the handed rays of the Aten with the long golden arms of the Vedic sun-god Surya. A means of transmission could have been the Indo-Iranian population of Mitanni (Thutmose IV has contracted a diplomatic marriage with a daughter of the Mitannian King Artatama). See Wallis Budge, Tutankhamen, Amenism, Atenism and Egyptian Monotheism (London: Hopkinson, 1932), and Harry R.H. Hall, The Ancient History of the Near East, (London: Methuen, 1952), 598-599.

[32] Aldred, Akhenaten, 194.

CHAPTER SIX

IN SEARCH

During the course of these essays, reference has been made intermittently to the matter of dogma or doctrine and its relation to more fundamental reality experienced. We have indicated some of the illustrative texts and provided a summary exposition and exegesis of a few of Voegelin's arguments regarding the genesis of the crisis of the age. The discovery of the symbolism of historiogenesis allowed Voegelin to integrate his understanding of the vast range of historical materials that lay at his disposition with the philosophical understanding of consciousness that he had developed. In the preceding chapter we examined in detail a specific example that illustrated both elements of Voegelin's new science. In this concluding chapter we would like to draw together some of the foregoing themes, beginning with a reconsideration of the question of dogma. Preeminently, it is the topic for which a hermeneutic of suspicion is most appropriate. A systematic exposition of Voegelin's account of reality, for which a hermeneutic of imaginative reconstitution or reminiscence is appropriate, must await another occasion. This concluding chapter may be considered as a restatement in Voegelinian terms of remarks made in the Introduction.

*

In his lecture on immortality, Voegelin began by
remarking that symbols were carriers of truth about
nonexistent reality.[1] The term, "nonexistent reality,"
is not widely used; we may say, however, that its negative
element indicates that nonexistent reality is distinct
from reality, the mode of being of which is existence in
space and time, or that comes into being and passes
away. Nonexistent reality is therefore not an object.
It is not for that reason subjective in the sense of
being an invention of the imagination. As a first approximation we may say that symbols convey meanings that are
experienced as real. At the same time however, the
mode of nonexistence characterizes the experience because
the experience is nothing more than consciousness of
participation in nonexistent reality. The symbolic artifacts --words, paintings, buildings, etc.-- exist, of
course, but the mode of being of meaning is nonexistent.
The meaning or the truth "is" only in the consciousness
of one who apprehends not the artifacts but the truth
they express; and the mode of being of this truth is
nonexistent, namely as consciousness of participation.
Anyone who has ever understood a poem has had this experience.

This somewhat peculiar language is clarified by
Voegelin's initial remarks in his "Equivalences" article.[2]
He began by noting the defective but intelligible language
that speaks of "values," especially of "permanent values."
Closer comparative inspection of historiogenetic texts,
of coronation ceremonies or of myths of judgement, to
name but three examples, indicates that we do not talk
of "values" at all but of "equivalent" texts, ceremonies,

myths. The comparison of the Sumerian King List with the issue at dispute between Voltaire and Bossuet could make sense because of a certain equivalence attaching not to the texts and the symbols they contain, but to the experiences that engendered the texts. "The language of 'equivalences', thus, implies the theoretical insight that not the symbols themselves but the constants of engendering experience are the true subject-matter of our studies."[3] The only permanence in history is man in search of his humanity and its order; there is nothing permanent about the symbols used to make sense of that search.

The absence of permanency does not, however, mean that we are adrift upon a sea of opinion, subjectivity and senseless flux, but it does mean that a discussion of equivalences involves a certain complexity. If the study is to do more than record the appearance of symbols and account for equivalent engendering experiences, it can do so only by way of symbols that are themselves engendered by the constants that undergird the disparate symbols and that the comparative study is attempting to account for. This means two things: first, the study of symbols is a reflective activity undertaken by one who is himself searching for the truth of the order of existence. Second, by searching for an account of equivalences, the searcher becomes aware of the time dimension in his search because he seeks to relate it to the searches of his predecessors. Accordingly, the searcher eventually must develop a philosophy of history, in the conventional sense of the term. The replacement of the defective language of "values" with the more adequate language of equivalences, Voegelin said, "marks the point at which the comparative study of symbols attains to an understanding of itself as a search of the search." The philosopher aware of his task as a search of the search exemplifies "the new historical consciousness."[4]

The search for the order of existence, we said, was the only permanence in history. If one takes up the search oneself and turns one's attention towards the reality identified as human existence, one encounters symbols concerned with the truth of existence that represent the experiences of one's predecessors. This array of symbols and experience is not an array of objects located as elements in a tradition. Indeed, because it is encountered as part of a search, the field will not look the same to everyone. This unavoidable fact leads to a radical problem of interpretation:

> what the philosopher moving in the field will see or not see, understand or not understand, or whether he will find his bearings in it at all, depends on the manner in which his own existence has been formed through intellectual discipline in openness towards reality, or deformed by his uncritical acceptance of beliefs which obscure the reality of immediate experience.[5]

One of the common deformations, which Voegelin occasionally identified as "school philosophy," is achieved by acquiescing in the opinion that the truth of existence is to be found in a set of propositions.

The motivation for the doctrinalization of the complex, experience-and-symbolization, may be found in the nonobjective or nonexistent mode of being of meaning and the accompanying intangibility of experience. The purpose of doctrine, as has been mentioned, was to protect experientially gained insights against false propositions. These sets of propositions are not so much wrong as deficient as compared to the full amplitude of experience of nonexistent reality. The deficiency consists in the attempt to use a language appropriate to the description of existent reality to describe nonexistent reality. The result is not simple untruth but dogmatic experience.

There follows a peculiar dialectic, some of the moments of which have been indicated incidentally in the preceeding chapters. Once the symbols that express the experiences of nonexistent reality are misunderstood as propositions referring to existing realities and objects of perception, one may sense the inapplicability or inappropriateness of the language. Looking for "permanent values," even the dogmatically deformed searcher "will find himself lost in the noisy struggle among the possessors of dogmatic truth --theological, or metaphysical, or ideological." A possible response is to regard the entire process of the search and not just its defective formulation with scepticism. "And we shall hardly blame him, if in the end he decides that scepticism is the better part of wisdom and becomes an honest relativist and historicist."[6] Scepticism, however, is simply an abstract negation of dogma, which is to say that it accepts the dogmatic definition of the topic. Intellectually, scepticism shares the belief that the field of symbols must be understood dogmatically. The political philosopher, however, denies this and points to the complex, reality experienced and symbolic articulation, as the proper subject matter for consideration --though the term "subject matter" is hardly the mot juste. But in response the sceptic can surely maintain that doctrinal conflict regarding the order of existence is far from being foreign to human history. Rather, it occupies a large place so that the sceptic can maintain that he is simply being a faithful empiricist.

To this observation, which the political philosopher would not deny as an observation, we are directed to the intellectual operations that account for its validity. They are comparatively straightforward. Deformed existence can be made the model of true existence; a competent philosopher with command of a sufficient range of historical materials who has acquiesced in the deformation of his own existence can deform the historical field of experience and symbolization by imposing on it his mode of deformation, which then will appear as true. Correspondingly, non-doctrinal sectors of reality are eclipsed by the symbolism that expresses the deformation.

The evidence that deformed existence can achieve such results seems clear enough; much of Chapter Three was concerned with the topic. The question then arises: how does history appear to the political philosopher whose consciousness is undeformed by dogma? The answer can be stated briefly because it has been presupposed in the initial analysis: doctrinaire existence is a

subfield within the horizon of reality experienced by
the political philosopher. The more comprehensive horizon
is shown to be more comprehensive because it includes
experienced realities, including nonexistent ones, that
are excluded by the defective doctrinal existence. This
"proof" will, of course, be valid only to non-doctrinal
consciousness, which raises the question of persuasion:
how does the political philosopher persuade the dogmatist?
As we shall see, the question is raised within the comprehensive context of reality itself. It is answered there
as well.

A negative indication, which demonstrates the
defectiveness of doctrinal existence, follows from the
fact that this deficient mode of understanding affects
the analytical operations of the person whose mind has
become doctrinaire. These defects may be pointed out
without too much trouble. Large blocks of From
Enlightenment to Revolution were devoted to just this
task. The problem for the doctrinaire existence is that,
while truth experienced can be excluded from the horizon
of doctrinal reality, it cannot be excluded from reality
as a whole. "When it is excluded from the universe of
intellectual discourse, its presence in reality makes
itself felt in the disturbance of mental operations."[7]
These mental operations have as their purpose the obscuring
of non-doctrinal realities. More broadly, the motive
for the act of deformation stems from the development
of centres of resistance to participating in reality,
including the reality of human existence.

Resistance to participation in reality and the cognitive eclipse of reality do not abolish it. Instead, reality remains present to consciousness --to deformed consciousness, in this case-- although its presence

> will now be marked by various indices of non-reality
> according to the character and degree of the distur-
> bance. For reality eclipsed but not abolished will
> exert a pressure to emerge into consciousness, and
> thereby to achieve full status of reality, that
> must be countered by acts of suppression.[8]

The ancillary symbols used to suppress the areas of friction between reality eclipsed and reality experienced in non-deformed consciousness constitute what Voegelin, following Robert Musil, called "second realities." The purpose of these imaginative dreams is to hide the conflict of the deformed with the non-deformed field of experience.

Deformed experience and its symbolization can be a pragmatic power in history just as easily as can non-deformed experience and its symbolization. Indeed, there is almost an engine within the economy of deformed existence that drives it towards power. The imaginative projections of second realities turn into political disturbances because the men whose consciousness is deformed by a refusal to participate in reality or to acknowledge it still must come to terms with reality in an underhanded way. They do so by continuing their refusal, but at the same time acknowledging it as a refusal by an act of will to make the world over so that it conforms to their particular second reality. The initial conflict with reality, Voegelin observed, "turns out to be a disturbance <u>within</u> reality."[9] At the same time, the pressure of reality exerts a force that resists the acts of deformation, not least of all in the actions of men who are not dreamers and whose consciousnesses are not deformed. This pragmatic resistance induces revisions into the projected second realities so that, in principle, there is no reason to expect the whole dreary business ever to grind to a halt. The succeeding generations of Marxists, positivists, and Freudians bear eloquent witness to the flexibility of the refusal to stop projecting.

What can be done, as Voegelin has done, is to subject the texts of the projectors of dream realities to analysis. Again, there are precedents for such analyses, from Aeschylus' and Plato's discussion of <u>nosos</u> to Musil. It is, in fact, one of the tasks of the political philosopher, a task undertaken in his demystifying mode. The analysis can be undertaken, furthermore, because the consciousness of the dreamer does not differ from that of the analyst: both distinguish between the dream and reality. The only difference between the two lies elsewhere, in the dreamer's belief in his power to transform reality. "The activist dreamer must know the trick-action, as distinguished from ordinary action, that will have the extraordinary result of transfiguring the nature of things. He must imagine himself to be a magician."[10] Again the evidence, which we surveyed in Chapter Three, is obvious enough.

Recast in the historiogenetic language of evolution, the symbolisms of antiquity that expressed the noetic and pneumatic experiences of faith and philosophy dried up into doctrines of supernatural revelation and natural reason, or "theology" and "metaphysics." Doctrinal conflicts underwent a further hardening and vulgarization as "religion" and "science." In Voegelin's words, "the doctrinaire theology and metaphysics of the eighteenth century were succeeded by the doctrinaire ideologies of the nineteenth and twentieth centuries; an older type of fundamentalist doctrine was followed by a new fundamentalism." The conflicting dogmas mark the era "roughly extending from 1750 to 1950" as "the age of modern dogmatomachy, frequently called the age of 'modern man'."[11] And modern man is characterized by the deformities just indicated.

So far as the political philosopher is concerned, whatever the catastrophes that have come from magical activists, there is nothing more to understand than "the phenomenon of a diseased consciousness which understands its own deformation as the possession of a magical power to transfigure reality."[12] The analysis of magic, of dream projects and second realities, is both a facing up to this peculiarity of the age and a way of resisting it.

*

It is possible to resist magic activism by understanding it for what it is. There are no laws of segmented history, for example, save in the fantasies of those who invent them for their own purposes.

History has no phases governed by states of consciousness, because there is no such thing as a
world-immanent consciousness that would politely
exclude this or that type of projection in obedience
to a doctrinaire's prescription. For History is
Man --not: the Doctrinaire-- written large; and
as man's consciousness is the reality of tension
toward the divine ground of his existence, history
is the struggle between existence in truth and the
deficient modes of existence.[13]

History must therefore be both a process of truth becoming
luminous in the experience of nonexistent reality and a
process of truth becoming deformed, dogmatized, and lost
or eclipsed. This insight contains the sobering implication that there "is no Archimedic point outside history
from which an exploration of existential consciousness
could be undertaken; there is no truth of existence
other than the truth emerging in the flux of presence."[14]
Because, therefore, images and symbols change historically
and are not permanent treasures of tradition and heritage,
the political philosopher is obliged to undertake meditative exploration of the structures of existential consciousness, which include experiences of nonexistent reality and its symbolization.

Consciousness, Voegelin just indicated, is the reality of tension toward the ground of existence.
Alternatively one might say that existence is structured
as a tension between truth and deformation of reality.
This structure is recognizably equivalent to the tensional
structure of history. In conclusion, we might indicate

a few things that may be said regarding that structure
or tension. These are no more than hints that, as I
have indicated, remain to be explored in detail.

Consciousness of tensional participation in reality
engenders symbols that express the experienced reality
of participation. Moreover, because those symbols articulate the experienced reality, they are part of the reality
symbolized. In particular, "the symbols consciousness,
experience, and symbolization denote the area where the
process of reality becomes luminous to itself." Voegelin
used the term "luminous" with respect to the truth of
reality experienced to indicate the nonobjective status
of participation. Cognition of participation

> becomes a luminosity in reality itself and, conse-
> quently, the knower and the known move into the
> position of tensional poles in a consciousness that
> we call luminous as far as it engenders the symbols
> which express the experience of its own structure.[15]

This reflective or meditative experience is recognizably
real just as the search of our philosophical predecessors
is recognizably equivalent to it.

Now, the reason one can say such things without
substituting the fallacy of a constant tension of existence
for the equally fallacious notion of permanent values
or some other doctrine of constants, is because the
notion of a "constant tension of existence" is
self-contradictory. The whole point about experience,
including the experience of tension, is that it is articulate only as equivalent symbolism. (Nothing can be said,

obviously, about experience that is not articulate, not even that it has occurred.) If there could be a constant experience, it would be articulate in a symbolism that claimed to be exempt from historical equivalence, which is impossible.

On the other hand, if we analyze the search for equivalent experiences engendering equivalent symbolisms, we are driven to conclude that the sought-for constant lies below the equivalent experiences that engender the equivalent symbolisms. This constant may be symbolized as the "depth," but "it does not furnish a substantive content in addition to our experiences of God, man, the world, and society, of existential tension, and of participation."[16] That is, the "depth" is not an area whose topography may be charted by various scientific discourses. Then, what is it? We have seen that it is not a reality experienced in addition to those just indicated. Nor is it a "perspective" on the field of reality as a whole; rather, it indicates, to use Plato's language in the Timaeus, the underlying reality that makes God and man, world and society, partners in a common order, the core experience of which is trust in the oneness of reality, in its coherence, lastingness, and intelligibility. "There is a depth below consciousness," Voegelin said, "but there is no depth below depth in infinite regress."[17] Accordingly, the depth yields up no permanent truths but only equivalent experiences of the primordial field of reality.

We may formulate this insight another way: there is no constant in history because the field of equivalent experiences and symbols is not an object or a collective phenomenon about which generalizations might be offered. New insights or new truths are not new realities superior in some way to old ones; they are superior insights into the same reality. What the search for constancy brings up from the depth is the process of reality in the mode of presence in consciousness that

> leaves a trail of equivalent symbols in time and space. To this trail we can, then, attach the conventional name of "history." History is not a given, as we have said, but a symbol by which we express our experience of the collective as a trail left by the moving presence of the process.[18]

But what of the process itself? It cannot be experienced except as presence, that is, concretely or really, in and by the consciousness of specific human beings. It cannot, therefore be experienced as a whole.

Even so, what is said of the process as a whole, even though experienced only as presence, is not sheer fantasy. We accept on faith the context of our concrete experience in search for truth. Why? Because the search for truth makes sense only if the truth concretely brought up from the depth is representative of the truth beyond the equivalent truth it expresses. "Behind every equivalent symbol in the historical field stands the man who has engendered it in the course of his search as representative of a truth that is more than equivalent."[19] The search itself renders equivalent truth, but it rests on the trust that, by searching, one participates representatively in a greater drama. About the end of the search nothing can be said. It is enough that Voegelin has indicated the end of man, namely the search for his humanity and its order.

NOTES

[1] Voegelin, "Immortality: Experience and Symbol."

[2] Voegelin, "Equivalences of Experience and Symbolization in History."

[3] Voegelin, "Equivalences," 215-16.

[4] Voegelin, Equivalences," 216.

[5] Voegelin, "Equivalences," 217.

[6] Voegelin, "Equivalences," 217.

[7] Voegelin, "Immortality," 254.

[8] Voegelin, "The Eclipse of Reality," 188.

[9] Voegelin, "Eclipse," 186/

[10] Voegelin, "Wisdom and the Magic of the Extreme: A Meditation," 243.

[11] Voegelin, "Equivalences," 219.

[12] Voegelin, "Wisdom and the Magic of the Extreme," 244.

[13] Voegelin, "Immortality," 256.

[14] Voegelin, "Wisdom and the Magic of the Extreme," 286.

[15] Voegelin, "Equivalences," 221.

[16] Voegelin, "Equivalences," 225.

[17] Voegelin, "Equivalences," 230.

[18] Voegelin, "Equivalences," 233.

[19] Voegelin, "Equivalences," 234.

APPENDIX

BIBLIOGRAPHY OF VOEGELIN'S WRITINGS

Contents
A. Primary Sources
        1.   Books
        2.   Articles and Essays
        3.   Book Reviews

B. Secondary Materials
        1.   Reviews and Notices

                a.   Ueber die Form des amerikanischen Geistes
                b.   Rasse und Staat
                c.   Die Rassenidee in der Geistesgeschichte
                d.   Der autoritaere Staat
                e.   Die politschen Relgionen
                f.   The New Science of Politics
                g.   Order and History
                h.   Science Politics and Gnosticism
                i.   Anamnesis
                j.   From Enlightenment to Revolution
                k.   Other Materials

        2.   Articles and Essays on Voegelin

A.   Primary Sources

   1.   Books

1928   Ueber die Form des amerikanischen Geistes.
          Tuebingen, J.C.B. Mohr. Pp. 246.

1933   Rasse und Staat. Tuebingen, J.C.B. Mohr.
          Pp. 227.

          Die Rassenidee in der Geistesgeschichte von
          Ray bis Carus. Berlin, Junker & Duennhaupt.
          Pp. viii plus 160.

1936   Der autoritaere Staat. Vienna, Springer.
          Pp. vii plus 289.

1938   Die politischen Religionen. Vienna,
          Berman-Fischer. Pp. 65; 2nd ed., with a new
          Preface, Stockholm, Berman-Fischer. Pp. 65.

1952   The New Science of Politics: An Introduction.
          Chicago, University of Chicago Press. Pp. xiii
          plus 193.

1956   Order and History, Vol. I: Israel and
          Revelation. Baton Rouge, Louisiana State
          University Press. Pp. xxv plus 533.

1957   Order and History, Vol. II: The World of
          the Polis. Baton Rouge, Louisiana State
          University Press. Pp. xvii plus 389.

          Order and History, Vol. III: Plato and
          Aristotle. Baton Rouge, Louisiana State
          University Press. Pp. xvii plus 383.

1959   Die Neue Wissenschaft der Politik/Eine
          Einfuehrung. Munich, Puste. Pp. 264.
          (Translation of The New Science of Politics,
          with a foreword to the German edition).

          Wissenschaft, Politik und Gnosis. Munich,
          Koesel. Pp. 93.

1966   Anamnesis: <u>Zur</u> <u>Theorie</u> <u>der</u> <u>Geschichte</u> <u>und</u>
        <u>Politik</u>. Munich, R. Piper & Co., Verlag.
        Pp. 395.

1968   <u>Science, Politics and Gnosticism</u>. Chicago,
        Henry Regnery. Pp. ix plus 114. (Translation
        of <u>Wissenschaft, Politik und Gnosis</u>, with a
        foreword to the American edition).

        <u>La Nuova Scienza politica</u>. Turin, Borla.
        Translation of <u>The New Science of Politics</u>,
        with an introduction by A. Del Noce, "Eric
        Voegelin e la critica dell 'idea di modernita'".

1970   <u>Il Mito del Mondo Nuovo</u>. Milan, Rusconi.
        (Translation of <u>Wissenschaft, Politik und
        Gnosis</u>, by Arnigio Munari, with an introducation
        by Mario Marcolla).

1972   Anamnesis: <u>Teoria della Storia e della
        Politica</u>. Milan, Giuffre. Translation of
        <u>Anamnesis</u>.

1974   <u>Order and History</u>, Vol. IV: <u>The Ecumenic
        Age</u>. Baton Rouge, Louisiana State University
        Press. Pp. xvii plus 340.

1975   <u>From Enlightenment to Revolution</u>. John H.
        Hallowell, ed. Durham, Duke University Press.
        Pp. ix plus 307.

1978   <u>Anamnesis</u>. Notre Dame, Notre Dame University
        Press. Partial Translation of <u>Anamnesis</u>, by
        Gerhart Niemeyer, with a new chapter,
        "Remembrance of Things Past".

1980   <u>Conversations with Eric Voegelin</u>. Eric
        O'Connor, ed., Montreal, Thomas More Institute.
        Pp. 154.

2.   <u>Articles and Essays</u>

1922   "Die gesellschaftliche Bestimmtheit
        soziologischer Erkenntnis," <u>Zeitschrift fuer</u>

Volkswirtschaft und Sozialpolitik, II: 4-6,
331-48.

1924   "Die Zeit in der Wirtschaft," Archiv fuer
Sozialwissenschaft und Sozialpolitik, LIII: 1,
186-211.

"Reine Rechtslehre und Staatslehre,"
Zeitschrift fuer oeffentliches Recht, IV: 1-2,
80-131.

1925   "Ueber Max Weber," Deutsche
Vierteljahresschrift fuer
Literaturwissenschaft und Geistes geschichte,
III: 2, 177-193.

1926   "Die Verfassungmaessigkeit des 18. Amendments
zur United States Constitution," Zeitschrift
fuer oeffentliches Recht, V: 3, 445-464.

"Wirtschafts- und Klassengegensatz in Amerika,"
Unterrichtsbriefe des Instituts fuer angewandte
Soziologie, V: 6, 6-11.

1927   "Zur Lehre von der Staatsform," Zeitschrift
fuer oeffentliches Recht, VI: 4, 572-608.

"Kelsen's Pure Theory of Law," Political Science
Quarterly, New York, Vol. XLII: 2, 268-276.

"La Follette und die Wisconsin-Idee,"
Zeitschrift fuer Politik, XVII: 4, 309-321.

1928   "Konjunkturforschung und Stabilisation des
Kapitalismus," Mitteilungen des Verbandes
oesterreichisher Banken und Bankiers, IX:
9-10, 252-259.

"Der Sinn der Erklaerung der Menschen- und
Buergerrechte von 1789," Zeitschrift fuer
oeffentliches Recht, VIII: 1, 82-120.

"Zwei Grundbergriffe der Humeschen
Gesellschaftslehre," Archiv fuer angewandte
Soziologie,, I: 2, 11-16.

"Die ergaezende Bill zum Federal Reserve Act
und die Dollarstabilisation," Mitteilungen des

Verbandes oesterreichischer Banken und
Bankiers, X: 11-12, 321-28.

"Die ergaenzende Bill zum Federal Reserve Act,"
Nationalwirtschaft, II: 2, 225-229.

1929   "Die Souveraenitaetstheorie Dickinsons und die
Reine Rechtslehre," Zeitschrift fuer
oeffentliches Recht, VIII: 3, 413-434.

"Die Transaktion," Archiv fuer angewandte
Soziologie, I: 4-5, 14-21.

1930   "Die amerikanische Theorie vom Eigentum,"
Archiv fuer angewandte Soziologie, II: 4,
165-172.

"Die amerikanische Theorie vom ordentlichen
Rechtsverfahren und von der Freiheit," Archiv
fuer angewandte Soziologie, III: 1, 40-57.

"Die oesterreichische Verfassungsreform von
1929," Zeitschrift fuer Politik, XIX: 9,
585-615.

"Max Weber," Koelner Vierteljahreshefte fuer
Soziologie, IX: 1-2, 1-16.

"Die Einheit des Rechts und das soziale
Sinngebilde Staat," Internationale Zeitschrift
fuer Theorie des Rechts, I: 2, 58-59.

1931   "Die Verfassungslehre von Carl Schmitt:
Versuch einer konstruktiven Analyse ihrer
staatstheoretischen Prinzipien," Zeitschrift
fuer oeffentliches Recht, XI: 1, 80-109.

"Das Sollen im System Kants," Gesellschaft,
Staat und Recht, Untersuchungen zur Reinen
Rechtslehre: Festschrift fuer Hans Kelsen zum
50. Geburtstag. ed. Alfred Verdrosz, Vienna,
Springer, 1931, 136-173.

1932   "Epilogue," to Ernst Dimnet's Die Kunst des
Denkens, Freiburg, Herder, 279-296.

1934   (With Adolf Merkl) "Le regime administratif.
Advantages et inconvenients," Memoires de

l'Academie Internationale de Droit comparé, II, 3. 126-149, Paris, Recueil Sirey.

1935   "Rasse und Staat," Psychologie des Gemeinschaftslebens, ed. Otto Klemm, Jena, Fischer, 91-104.

1936   "Volksbildung, Wissenschaft und Politik," Monatsschrift fuer Kultur und Politik, I: 7, 594-603.

"Josef Relich," Juristisch Blaetter, LXV: 23, 485-6.

1937   "Das Timurbild der Humanisten: Eine Studie zur politischen Mythenbildung," Zeitschrift fuer oeffentliches Recht, Vienna, Springer, XVII: 5, 554-582. Reprinted in Anamnesis, 153-78.

(With Otto Brunner & Gregor Sebba) "Changes in the Ideas on Government and Constitution in Austria since 1918," Austrian Memorandum No. 3. International Studies Conference on Peaceful Change, Paris. League of Nations, Institute for International Intellectual Cooperation.

1940   "Extended Strategy: A New Technique of Dynamic Relations," The Journal of Politics, II: 3.

"The Growth of the Race Idea," The Review of Politics, II: 3, 283-317.

1941   "Some Problems of German Hegemony," The Journal of Politics, III: 2, 154-168.

"The Mongol Orders of Submission to European Powers, 1245-1255," Byzantion, XV, 378-413.

1942   "The Theory of Legal Science: A Review," Louisiana Law Review, IV, 554-572.

1944   "Nietzsche, the Crisis and the War," The Journal of Politics, VI: 2, 177-212.

"Siger de Brabant," Philosophy and Phenomenologial Research, IV: 4, 505-526.

"Political Theory and the Pattern of General History," The American Political Science Review, XXXVIII: 4, 746-754. Reprinted in Ernest S. Griffith, ed. Research in Political Science. Chapel Hill, University of North Carolina Press 1948. 190-201.

1946   "Bakunin's Confession," The Journal of Politics, VIII: 1, 24-43.

1947   "Zu Sanders 'Allgemeine Staatslehre'," Oesterreichische Zeitschrift fuer oeffentliches Recht, New Series, I: 1-2, 103-135.

"Plato's Egyptian Myth," The Journal of Politics, IX: 3, 307-324.

1948   "The Origins of Scientism," Social Research, XV: 4, 462-494; Translation, "Wissenschaft als Aberglaube/Die Urspruenge des Scientifismus," Wort und Wahrheit, VI: 5 (1951), 341-360.

1949   "The Philosophy of Existence: Plato's Gorgias," The Review of Politics, XI: 4, 477-498.

1950   "The Formation of the Marxian Revolutionary Idea," The Review of Politics, XII, 3, 275-302; Translation, "La Formacion de la idea revolucionaria marxista," Hechos e Ideas, Buenos-Aires, XII, 1951, XXII, 227-250 and "La formazione della idea marxiana di rivoluzione," Caratteri Gnostici della Modernita politica, economica, e sociale. G. Gorghi, ed. Rome, Carteggi, 1980, 81-130. Reprinted in The Image of Man, ed. M.A. Fitzsimmons, T. McAvoy, Frank O'Malley. Notre Dame, University of Notre Dame, 1959. 65-281.

1951   "Machiavelli's Prince: Background and Formation," The Review of Politics, XIII: 2, 142-168.

"More's Utopia," Oesterreichische Zeitschrift fuer oeffentliches Recht, New Series, III: 4, 451-468.

1952   "Gnostische Politik," Merkur, IV: 4, 301-317.
        Translation, "Politica Gnostica," Trascendenza
        e Gnosticismo in Eric Voegelin. G. Borghi,
        ed. Rome, Carteggi, 1979, 137-75.

        "Goethe's Utopia," Goethe after Two Centuries,
        ed. Carl Hammer, Baton Rouge, Louisiana State
        University Press. 55-62.

1953   "The Origins of Totalitarianism," The Review
        of Politics, XV: 1, 68-85, with a reply by
        Hannah Arendt.

        "The World of Homer," The Review of Politics,
        XV: 4, 491-523.

        "The Oxford Political Philosophers," The
        Philosophical Quarterly, III: 11, 97-114;
        Translation, "Philosophie der Politik in
        Oxford," Philosophische Rundschau, I: 1
        (1953-4), 23-48.

1956   "Necessary Moral Bases for Communication in a
        Pluralistic Society," in Problems of
        Communication in a Pluralistic Society.
        Milwaukee, Marquette University Press. 53-68.

1958   "Der Prophet Elias," Hochland, L: 4, 325-339.

1959   "Diskussionsbereitschaft," Erziehung zur
        Freiheit. Albert Hunold, ed. Erlenbach-Zurich
        und Stuttgart, Rentsch, 355-372; Translation,
        "On Readiness to Rational Discussion," Freedom
        and Serfdom. Albert Hunold, ed.
        Dordrecht-Holland, D. Reidel Publishing Co.,
        1961. 269-284.

        "Demokratie im neuen Europa," Gesellschaft
        Staat-Erziehung, IV: 7, 293-300. Reprinted
        in Akademie fuer Politische Bildung, 25 Jahre
        Akadamie fuer Politische Bildung. Tutzing,
        1982, 20-31.

1960   "El concept de la 'buena sociedad'," Cuadernos
        del Congresso por la Libertad de la Cultura,
        Suplemento del No. 40, 25-28.

"Religionsersatz/Die gnostischen Massen bewegunen unserer Zeit," Wort und Wahrheit, XV: 1, 5-18. Translation included in Science, Politics & Gnosticism, 81-114.

"La Societé industrielle à la recherche de la raison," Colloques de Rheinfelden, ed. Raymond Aron, George Kennan, et al. Paris, Calmann-Levy, 1960, 44-64; Translation, Die industrielle Gesellschaft auf der Suche nach der Vernunft, Das Seminar von Rheinfelden; Gesellschaft und die drei Welten, Zurich, EVZ-Verlag, 1961, 46-64; Translation, "Industrial Society in Search of Reason," in World Technology and Human Destiny, R. Aron, ed. Ann Arbor, University of Michigan Press, 1963. 31-46.

"Verantwortung und Freiheit in Wirtschaft und Demokratie," Die Aussprache, Bonn, X: 6, 207-213.

"Der Liberalismus und seine Geschichte," Christentum und Liberalismus, Studien und Berichte der Katholischen Akademie in Bayern, XIII, Karl Forster, ed. Munich, Zink, 1960, 13-42; Translation, "Liberalism and its History," The Review of Politics, XXXVI: 4, 504-520.

"Historiogenesis," Philosophisches Jahrbuch LXVIII and in Philsophia Viva: Festschrift fuer Alois Dempf, ed. Max Mueller and Michael Schmaus, Freiburg/Munich, Alber, 1960, 419-446; Reprinted in Anamnesis, 79-116; Translated and Expanded, The Ecumenic Age, ch. 1, 59-114.

1961   "Toynbee's History as a Search for Truth," The Intent of Toynbee's History. Edward T. Gargan, ed. Chicago, Loyola University Press, 1961, 181-198.

"Les perspectives d'avenir de la civilisation occidentale," L'Histoire et ses Interpretations: Entretiens autour de Arnold Toynbee, R. Aron, ed. The Hague, Mouton, 1961, 133-151.

1962   "World Empire and the Unity of Mankind,"
        International Affairs, XXXVIII, 170-188.

1963   "Das Rechte von Natur," Oesterreichische
        Zeitschrift fuer oeffentliches Recht, XIII:
        1-2, 38-51; Reprinted in Anamnesis, 117-133.

        "History and Gnosis," Bernard Anderson, ed.,
        The Old Testament and Christian Faith. New
        York, Harper & Row. 64-89. Translation in
        Anamnesis, 116-140.

1964   "Ewiges Sein in der Zeit," Zeit und Geschichte:
        Dankesgabe an Rudolph Bultmann Zum 80.
        Geburtstag, ed. Erich Dinkler, Tuebingen,
        J.C.B. Mohr (Paul Siebeck). 591-614;
        Reprinted in Anamnesis, 254-280.

        "Der Mensch in Gesellschaft und Geschichte,"
        Oesterreichische Zeitschrift fuer
        oeffentliches Recht, XIV, 1-2, 1-13.
        Translation in Caratteri gnostici della Moderna
        Politica, economica e sociale.

        "Demokratie und Industriegesellschaft," Die
        Unternehmerische Verantwortung in unserer
        Gesellschaftsordnung, vol. IV of the
        Walter-Raymond-Stiftung meeting (Cologne and
        Opladen, Westdeutscher Verlag), 96-114.
        Translation in Caraterri gnostici della Moderna
        Politica, economica e sociale.

        "Metaphysik und Geschichte" in Die Philosophie
        und die Frage nach dem Fortschritt. Munich,
        Pustet, 11-23.

1965   "Was ist Natur?," Historica, Festschrift fuer
        Friedrich Engel-Janosi. H. Hantsch, F
        Valsecchi, E. Voegelin, eds. Vienna, Herder,
        1-18; Reprinted in Anamnesis, 134-152;
        translated in Anamnesis, 71-88.

1966   "Die deutsche Universitaet und die Ordnung der
        deutschen Gesellschaft," Die Deutsche
        Universitaet im Dritten Reich. Ludwig Kotter,
        ed. Munich, Piper 241-282. Reprinted as
        "Universitaet und Oeffentlichkeit: Zur

Pneumopathologie der Deutschen Gesellschaft,"
Wort und Wahrheit 8/9 (1966), 497-518.

"Was ist politische Realitaet?" Politische
Vierteljahresschrift 7, 2-54. Expanded in
Anamnesis, 283-354; translated in Anamnesis,
143-213.

1967   "On Debate and Existence," The Intercollegiate
Review, III: 4-5, 143-152.

"Immortality: Experience and Symbol," Harvard
Theological Review, LX: 3, 235-279.

"Apocalisse e rivoluzione," Caratteri gnostici
della Modernita Politica, economica e sociale,
45-79.

1968   "Configurations in History," The Concept of
Order. Paul Kuntz, ed. Seattle, University
of Washington Press, 23-42. Translation in
Transcendenza e Gnosticismo, 95-135.

"Zur Geschichte des politischen Denkens" in
Zwischen Revolution und Restauration:
Politisches Denken in England im 17
Jahrhunderts. Munich, List, 63-97.

"Helvetivs," Arno Baruzzi, ed. Aufklaerung
und Materialismus im Frankreich des 18.
Jahrhunderts. Munich, List, 63-97.

1970   "Equivalences of Experience and Symbolization
in History," Eternita e Storia, I valori
permanenti nel divenire storico, Firenze,
Valecchi, 215-234. Reprinted with minor
changes in Philosophical Studies XXVIII (1981),
88-103.

"The Eclipse of Reality," Phenomenology and
Social Reality. Maurice Natanson, ed.
(Memorial volume for Alfred Schutz). The Hague,
Martinus Nijhoff, 185-194.

1971   "Henry James' 'The Turn of the Screw'," 1.
Prefatory note by Donald E. Stanford; 2.
Foreword by Robert Heilman, 3. A letter to
Robert Heilman, 4. Postscript: "On Paradise

and Revolution," The Southern Review, New Series, VII: 1, 3-67.

"The Gospel and Culture," Jesus and Man's Hope, vol. II. D. Miller and D.G. Hadidian, ed. Pittsburgh, Pittsburgh Theological Seminary Press, 59-101.

"On Hegel: A Study in Sorcery," Studium Generale, XXIV, 335-368.

1973   "On Classical Studies," Modern Age, XVII, 2-8.

"Philosophies of History," New Orleans Review, II, 135-9.

1974   "Reason: The Classic Experience," The Southern Review, New Series, X: 2, 237-264. Reprinted in Anamnesis, 89-115; translated in Trascendenza e Gnosticismo, 41-93.

1975   "Response to Professor Altizer's 'A New History and a New but Ancient God,'" Journal of the American Academy of Religion, XLIII: 4, 765-772.

1977   "Remembrance of Things Past," in Anamnesis 3-13.

1981   "Two Letters to Alfred Schutz," Peter Opitz and Gregor Sebba, eds. The Philosophy of Order. Stuttgart, Klett-Cotta, 449-65.

"Der Meditative Ursprung philosophischen Ordnungswissens," Zeitschrift fuer Politik, 28, 130-37.

"Wisdom and The Magic of the Extreme: A Meditation," The Southern Review 17, 235-87.

1982   "The American Experience," Modern Age, 26, 332-33.

"Epilogue," Ellis Sandoz, ed. Eric Voegelin's Thought: A Critical Appraisal. Durham, Duke University Press. 199-202.

3. Book Reviews

F. Kaufmann, Logik und Rechtswissenschaft,
Zeitschrift fuer oeffentliches Recht, 3 (1923),
707-8.

C. Schmidt, Verfassungslehre, Zeitschrift fuer
oeffentliches Recht, 11 (1931), 89-109.

K. Hermann, Die Grundlagen des oeffentlichen Rechts,
Zeitschrift fuer oeffentliches Recht, 12 (1932),
630-1.

F.W. Jerusalem, Gemeinschaft und Staat, Zeitschrift
fuer oeffentliches Recht 13 (1933) 764.

M. Rumpf, Politische und soziologische Staatslehre,
Zeitschrift fuer oeffentliches Recht, 14 (1934),
268-9.

D. Schindler, Verfassung und soziale Struktur,
Zeitschrift fuer Oeffentliches Recht, 14 (1934),
256-7.

A.E. Zimmern, Nationality and Government, and The
Prospects of Democracy, Zeitschrift fuer
Oeffentliches Recht, 14 (1934), 269.

A.E. Hoche, Das Rechtsgefuehl in Justiz und Politik,
Zeitschrift fuer Oeffentliches Recht, 14 (1934)
270-1.

A. Schutz, Der Sinnhafte Aufbau der sozialen Welt,
Zeitschrift fuer Oeffentliches Recht, 14 (1934),
668-72.

H. Krupka, Carl Schmitts Theorie des "Politischen,"
Zeitschrift fuer Oeffentliches Recht, 17 (1937),
665.

B. Horvath, Rechtssoziologie, Zeitschrift fuer
Oeffentliches Recht, 17 (1937), 667-71.

P. Berger, Faschismus und Nationalsozialismus,
Zeitschrift fuer Oeffentliches Recht, 17 (1937),
671-2.

G. Mosca, The Ruling Class, Journal of Politics I (1939), 434-36.

"Right and Might" review of James Brown Scott, Law, the State and the International Community, Review of Politics, III (1941), 122-123.

"Two Recent Contributions to the Science of Law," review of N.S. Timasheff, Introduction to the Sociology of Law and Edgar Bodenheimer, Jurisprudence, Review of Politics, III (1941), 399-404.

M. Y. Sweezy, Structure of the Nazi Economy and E. Fraenkel, The Dual State, Journal of Politics IV (1942), 269-272.

John Hallowell, The Decline of Liberalism, Journal of Politics VI (1944), 107-109.

Count Carlo Sforza, Contemporary Italy: Its Intellectual and Moral Origins, tr., D. and D. De Kay, Journal of Politics, VII (1945), 94-97.

Fred L. Schuman, Soviet Politics, At Home and Abroad, Journal of Politics, VIII (1946), 212-220.

G. Eisler, et al., The Lessons of Germany, American Political Science Review XL (1946), 385-386.

F. Sanders, Allgemeine Staatslehre, Oesterreichische Zeitschrift fuer Oeffentliches Recht, I (1946), 106-35.

Rudolph Schlesinger, Soviet Legal Theory: Its Social Background and Development, Journal of Politics, IX (1947), 129-131.

D. Fellman, ed., Post-War Governments of Europe, American Political Science Review XLI (1947), 595-596.

E. Cassirer, The Myth of the State, Journal of Politics IX (1947), 445-447.

J. Huizinga, Homo Ludens, Journal of Politics, X (1948), 179-187.

L. Strauss, On Tyranny, Review of Politics XI (1949), 241-244.

John Bowle, Western Political Thought, Review of Politics XI (1949), 262-263.

P. G. Bergin and M. A. Fisch, trs. Vico, The New Science, Catholic Historical Review XXXV (1949-1950), 75-6.

F. Wagner, Geschichtswissenschaft, American Political Science Review XLVII (1953), 261-262.

Wild, Plato's Modern Enemies and Levinson, in Defence of Plato, American Political Science Review XLVIII (1954), 859-862.

R. Polin, Politique et Philosophie chez Thomas Hobbes, American Political Science Review XLIX (1955), 597-598.

B.   Secondary Materials

   1.   Reviews, Notices, and Review Articles

a.   Ueber die Form des amerikanischen Geistes

L. Pitamic, Oesterreichische Zeitschrift fuer offentliches Recht, VIII, (1928-1929), 637-639.

M. Palvi, Archiv fuer Rechts und Wirtschaftsphilosophie, XXII (1929), 645-47.

Ch. Lutkens, Archiv fuer Sozialwissenschaft und Sozialpolitik, LXII (1929), 615.

Fr. Schonemann, Literatur Zeitung, VI (1929), 1258.

Savermann, Nationalwirtschaft, II (1929), 666.

C. Brinkmann, Historische Zeitschrift, CXL (1929), 109-111.

Louis Wirth, American Journal of Sociology, XXXVI (1931), 681.

W. Gerloff, Vergangenheit und Gegenwart, LIV (1931), 452-4.

Anon, Bookman, (London) IV (1933), 19-20.

b.   Rasse und Staat

N. Guerke, Deutsche Literatur-Zeitung, IV (1933), 2196-98.

N. Guerke, Verwaltungs-Blatt, LIV (1933), 781-85.

E.   Rasch, Koelnische Zeitung, 18 June 1933.

Anon, Kreuz-Zeitung, (Berlin) 2 September 1933.

We.   Muhlmann,   Archiv   fuer   Rassen   und Gesellschaftsbiologie, XXVII (1934), 431-433.

Anon, Juristische Blaetter, LXIII (1934), 287.

E.   Geyer,   Mitteilungen   der   Anthropologischen Gesellschaft, LXIV (1934), 339.

N. Plessner, Zeitschrift fuer oeffentliches Recht, XIV (1934), 407.

E.C.   Hughes,   American   Journal   of   Sociology,   XL (1934), 377-78.

G.   Richard, Nouvelle revue de Hongrie, XLII (1935), 73-75.

Anon, Buecherkunde der Reichsstelle zur Foerderung des deutschen Schriftums, II (1935), 31.

G.A.   Lutterbeck,   Stimme   der   Zeit,   CXXIX   (1935), 68.

Anon, Zeitschriftenverlagen der Bad Charlottenburg, XXXVIII (1936), 306.

E.   Brehier, La Revue critique d'histoire et de littérature, New Series, C (1939), 367-8.

c. Die Rassenidee in der Geistesgeschichte von Ray
bis Carus

L. von Renthe-Fink, Berliner Boersenzeitig, 25 March
1933.

V. Lebzelter, Blaetter fuer deutsche Philosophie,
VIII (1934), 192-93.

Ungerer, Kantstudien, XXXIX (1934), 371-73.

M. Muckermann, Nassovia und Schrittum, (1934) 3/4.

L. Glaser, Schoenere Zukuntt, (Vienna) 9-10, (1934)
801.

Anon, Germanien: Blaetter fuer Freunde germanische
Vorgeschichte, (Leipzig) (1935), 317.

M. Hesch, Vergangenheit und Gegenwart, XXV (1935),
627.

Anon, Vierteljahreschrift fuer Sozial und
Wirtschaftsgeschichte, XXVIII (1935), 55.

P. Brohmer, Zeitschritt fuer deutsche Bildung, XI,
(1935), 330.

H. Amberger, Die Sonne, XIII (1936), 371.

Anon, Hochkirche, (Munich) XIX (1937), 183.

K. Rosenfelder, Nordische Stimmen, (Erfurt) V
(1939), 109.

d. Der Autoritaere Staat

F. Adler, Prager juristische Zeitschrift, XI (1936),
745.

A. Perkmann, Monatsschritt fuer Kultur und Politik,
(Nov. 1936), 1041.

F. Sander, Prager juristische Zeitschrift, XVII
(1937), 278.

A. Lenz, Zeitschrift fuer oeffentliches Recht, XVII
(1937), 258.

B. Dungern, Historische Zeitschrift, CLVII (1937),
152.

O. Rabl, Historische Vierteljahreschrift, XXXI
(1937), 397-406.

John Brown Mason, American Sociological Review, II
(1937), 579-80.

A. Meyendorff, Political Science Quarterly, LIII
(1937), 478-9.

L. Legaz, Universidad, (Saragossa) XIV (1937), 594.

e.   Die politischen Religionen

R.H. Williams, American Sociological Review, VI
(1941), 402-4.

f.   The New Science of Politics

Anon, Ethica, VII (1968), 156-157.

John Hallowell, Louisiana Law Review, XIII (1952-53),
525-30.

William Anderson, Journal of Politics, XV (1953), 563-568.

Hans Aufricht "A Restatement of Political Theory: A
Note on Eric Voegelin's New Science of Politics,"
Western Political Quarterly, VI (1953), 458-468.

A. Brecht, Annals, CCLXXXVIII (1953), 215-16.

_____, Social Research, XX (1953), 230-235.

J.H. Franklin, Political Science Quarterly, LXVIII
(1953), 157-158.

Alan Gerwirth, Ethics, LXIII (1953), 142-144.

A. Harrigan, Christian Century, LXX (1953), 386.

Hans Kohn, The Nation, CLXXVI (Jan. 17, 1953), 57.

Bernard Wand, Philosophical Review, LXII (1953), 608-609.

F.G. Wilson, American Political Science Review, XLVII (1953), 542-543.

J.S. Roucek, American Sociological Review, XIX (1954), 494-495.

Anon, Times Literary Supplement, (August 7, 1953), 504.

Anon, US Book Quarterly Book Review, IX (March, 1953), 71.

Martin Wright, International Affairs, XXXI (1955), 336-337.

Robert Dahl, World Politics, VII (1955), 479-489.

J.F. Fueyo, "Eric Voegelin y su Reconstruccion de la Ciencia Politica" Rivista de Estudios Politicos, LXXIX (1955), 67-116.

H.J. Muller, "Shuddering Before the Mystery," New Republic, CXXIV (1956), 19-20.

L.C. McDonald, "Voegelin and the Positivists: A New Science of Politics?" Midwest Journal of Political Science, III (1957), 233-51.

g.   Order and History

E.O. James, Order and History I, The Hibbert Journal, LV (1956), 408-410.

H.J. Miller, Order and History I, New Republic, CXXXV (Oct. 29, 1956), 19-20.

J. De Fraine, Order and History I, Bijdrajen (Maastricht), XVIII (1957), 78.

E.J. Fisher, Order and History I, Annals, CCCX (1957), 233.

J. Fohren, "Israel's Staatzordnung im Rahmen des Alten
    Orients," Zeitschrift fuer Oeffentliches Recht VIII
    (1957), 129-148.

Moshe Greenburg, Order and History I, American Political
    Science Review, LI (1957), 1101-1103.

S. Hooke, Order and History I, The Society for Old
    Testament Study Booklist, (1957), 57f.

Gerhardt Niemeyer, Order and History I, Review of Politics,
    XIX (1957), 403-409.

H.H. Rowley, Order and History I, Journal of Biblical
    Literature, LXXVI (1957), 157-158.

H.J. Schoeps, Order and History I, Historische
    Zeitschrift, CLXXXIV (1957), 606-607.

R.L. Shinn, Order and History I, Christian Century, LXXIV
    (1957), 894.

A.-H. Chroust, Order and History II, The Thomist, XXI
    (1957), 381-391.

R.L. Horn, Order and History I, Union Theological Seminary
    Quarterly, XII (1957), 65-7.

Russell Kirk, "Behind the Veil of History", Order and
    History I, (1957), 466-476.

J.B. Pritchard, Order and History I, American Historical
    Review, LXIII (1957-1958), 640-641.

C.A. Robinson, Order and History II-III, American
    Historical Review, LXIII (1957-1958), 939-941.

J.A. Marks, Order and History I, Theology Today, XV (1958),
    266-269.

R. Martin-Achard, Order and History I, Theologische
    Zeitschrift, XIV (1958), 138-139.

J. Mauchline, Order and History I, Journal of Semitic
    Studies, III (1958), 179-181.

J. Walgrave, Order and History I, Tijdschrift voor
    Philosophie, XX (1958), 358-363.

R.L. Shinn, Order and History II, Christian Century, LXXV (1958), 1053.

R.L. Shinn, Order and History II, Saturday Review, XLI (March 8, 1958), 27.

E.L. Ehrlich, Order and History I, Zeitschrift fuer Religions- und Geistesgeschichte, X (1958), 295-296.

T. Berry, Order and History I-III, Thought, XXXIII (1958), 273-78.

F. Engel-Janosi, Order and History I-III, Wort und Wahrheit, XIII (1958), 538-544.

Moses Hadas, Order and History I-III, Journal of the History of Ideas, XIX (1958), 442-444.

Trusdell S. Brown, Order and History I-III, Annals, CCCIX (1958), 187-188.

Stanley Rosen, Order and History II-III, Review of Metaphysics, XII (1958), 257-276.

S. Laver, Order and History II-III, Journal of Jewish Studies, IX (1958), 107-108.

Harold Fisch, Order and History I, Journal of Jewish Studies, IX (1958), 203-204.

H. Hummel, Order and History I, Concordia Theological Review, XXIX (1958), 395-6.

R.M. Achard, Order and History I, Theologische Zeitschrift XIV (1958), 138-9.

Harry S. Gehman, Order and History I, Interpretation: A Journal of Bible and Theology, XII (1958), 318-321.

F.D. Wilhelmsen, Order and History I, The Modern Age, III (1958-1959), 182-189.

Peter Stanlis, Order and History II-III, The Modern Age, III (1958-1959), 189-196.

Robert Ammerman, Order and History II-III, Philosophy and Phenomenological Research, XIX (1958-1959), 539-540.

Anon, Order and History I, Revue de Metaphysique et de Morale, LXIV (1959), 501.

Victor Ehrenberg, Order and History II, Historische Zeitschrift, CLXXXVII (1959), 369-373.

H.H. Scullard, Order and History I-III, History, XLIV (1959), 33-34.

G.B. Kerferd, Order and History II-III Classical Review, IX (1959), 251-252.

G. Neimeyer, Order and History II-III, Review of Politics, XXI (1959), 589-596.

Edouard Will, Order and History II-III, Revue de Philologie, 3rd series, XXXIII (1959), 97-98.

Cherniss, H., "Plato 1950-1957," includes Order and History III, Lustrum, V (1960), 445.

H. Kuhn, Order and History III, Historische Zeitschrift, CXCI (1960), 360-364.

Whitney J. Oates, Order and History III, Classical Journal, LVI (1960), 90-92.

N.W. Porteous, Order and History I-III, English Historical Review, LXXV (1960), 288-290.

R. Weil, Order and History II-III, Revue des Etudes grecques, LXXIII (1960), 547-548.

J.M. Mavchline, Order and History II-III, Journal of Semitic Studies, V (1960), 84-5.

William F. Albright, Order and History I, Theological Studies, XXII (1961), 270-279. Reprinted in History, Archeology and Christian Humanism. London, Black, 1965.

Robert S.J. North, Order and History I, Bibliotheca Orientalis, XVIII (1961), 85-87.

Ellis Sandoz, Order and History I-III, Social Research, XXVIII (1961), 229-234.

A.W.H. Adkins, Order and History II-III, Journal of Hellenic Studies, LXXXI (1961), 192-193.

Martin R.P. MacGuire, Order and History I-III, Catholic Historical Review, XLVIII (1962-1963), 410-412.

Robert C. Denton, Order and History I, Anglican Theological Review, XLVI (1965), 321.

Pierre Hassner, Order and History I-III, Revue français de Science politique, X (1968), 713-15.

B.W. Anderson, "Politics and the Transcendent: Eric Voegelin's Philosophical and Theological Analysis of the Old Testament in the Context of the Ancient Near East," Political Science Reviewer, I (1971), 1-30.

James L. Wiser, "Philosophy and Human Order", Order and History II, Political Science Reviewer, II (1972), 137-61.

Frederick D. Wilhelmsen, Order and History IV, Triumph, X:1 (1975), 32-35.

Gregor Sebba, "Eric Voegelin: From Enlightenment to Universal Humanity" Order and History IV, The Southern Review, N.S. XI (1975), 918-925.

Dante Germino, Order and History IV, Journal of Politics, XXXVII (1975), 847-48.

Thomas Molnar, "Voegelin as Historian" Order and History IV The Modern Age, XIX (1975), 427-429.

Ivo Thomas, Order and History IV, American Journal of Jurisprudence, XX (1975), 168-169.

Anon, Order and History IV, History: Reviews of New Books, III (Aug., 1975), 233.

Thomas J.J. Altizer, "A New History and a New but Ancient God? A Review Essay" Order and History IV, Journal of the American Academy of Religion, XLIII (1975), 757-764.

Anon, Order and History IV, Christian Century, XLII (March 19, 1975), 291.

John Kirby, Order and History IV, Canadian Journal of
    Political Science, IX (1975), 363-4.

Bruce Douglass, Order and History IV, Christian Century,
    III (Feb. 18, 1976), 155-156.

William Havard, Order and History IV, American Historical
    Review, LXXXI:3 (1976), 557-8.

Anon, Order and History IV, Virginia Quarterly Review,
    LII (1976), 43.

Bruce Douglass, "The Break in Voegelin's Program" Order
    and History IV , Political Science Reviewer, VII
    (1977), 1-22.

Dante Germino, "Eric Voegelin's Framework for Political
    Evaluation in his Recently Published Work," American
    Political Science Review, LXXII (1978), 110-21.

h.   Science, Politics and Gnosticism

Alan Bloom, American Political Science Review, LIV (1960),
    226-227.

E. Sandoz, Intercollegiate Review, V:2 (1968-1969),
    117-123.

E. Sandoz, National Review, XXI (Jan. 14, 1969), 32-33.

Thomas Molnar, Modern Age, XIV (1970), 334-337.

Massimo Corsale, Rivista internazionale di Filosofia del
    Dritto, XLVIII (1971), 195-6.

Franco Pistoia, Giornale di Metafisica, XXVI (1971),
    538-9.

F.H. Rivero, Rivista Venozolana de Filosofia, I (1973),
    135-138.

i.   Anamnesis

A. Dempf, Philosophisches Jahrbuch, LXXIV (1966-7), 405-6.

J. Freund, Revue de Metaphysique et de Morale, LXXIII (1968),

G. Neimeyer, Review of Politics, XXX (1968), 259-72. 386-7.

Klaus J. Hermann, Canadian Journal of Political Science, III (1970), 492-4.

Dante Germino, "Eric Voegelin's Anamnesis," Southern Review, VII (1971), 68-88.

E. Sandoz, "The Foundation of Voegelin's Political Theory," Political Science Reviewer I (1971), 30-73.

D'Agostino, Rivista internazionale di Filosofia del Dritto, L (1973), 576-7.

G.L. Galgan, Library Journal, CIII (1978), 1064.

Thomas J.J. Altizer, Journal of Religion, LIX (1979), 375-6.

Anon, Choice XV (1979), 1536.

j.   From Enlightenment to Revolution

Anon, History: Reviews of New Books, III (1975), 206.

Anon, Choice, XII (Nov. 1975), 1186.

Dante Germino, National Review, XXVII (1975), 1185-6.

Ellis Sandoz, Western Political Quarterly, XXVIII (1975), 744-5.

John Kirby Canadian Journal of Political Science, IX (1975), 363-4.

Gregor Sebba, "Eric Voegelin: From Enlightenment to
Universal Humanity," Southern Review, XI (1975),
918-25.

Thomas Molnar, "Voegelin as Historian," The Modern Age,
XIX (1975), 427-29.

Miles Morgan Journal of Politics, XXXVIII (1976), 191.

Gerald Cavanaugh, American Historical Review, LXXXI:2

Peter Widulsky, Aitia, III (1976), 25-29.

Thomas Pangle, Political Theory, IV (1976), 104-8.

James L. Wiser, Thought, LII (1977), 214-15.

Barry Cooper, "A Fragment from Eric Voegelin's History
of Western Political Thought," Political Science
Reviewer, VII (1977), 23-52.

John Gueguen, "Voegelin's From Enlightenment to
Revolution," The Thomist XL:1 (1978), 123-34.
(1976), 358.

Dante Germino, "Eric Voegelin's Framework for Political
Evaluation in his Recently Published Work," American
Political Science Review, LXXII (1978), 110-21.

k.   Other Materials

H. Arendt, Reply to Voegelin's review of Origins of
Totalitarianism , Review of Politics, XV (1953),
76-84.

Leo Strauss, 'Restatement on Xenophon's Hiero' in What
Is Political Philosophy? and Other Studies, Glencoe,
The Free Press, 1959, 96-103. Reprinted in Leo
Strauss, On Tyranny, rev. ed., Ithaca, Cornell
University Press, 1963, 190-197.

Steven Muller, Review of Festgabe fuer Eric Voegelin,
American Political Science Review, LVI (1963),
967-968.

David Noel Freedman, Review of Anderson, Old Testament and Christian Faith on Voegelin's "History and Gnosis", Theology Today, XXI (1964), 225-228.

H.R. Schlette, Review of Festgabe fuer Eric Voegelin, Hochland: Monatsschrifte fuer alle Gebiete des Wissens, LVII (1964), 83-87.

J. Barr, Review of Anderson, Old Testament and Christian Faith on Voegelin's "History and Gnosis", Interpretation: A Journal of Bible and Theology, XIX (1965), 217-220.

B. Orchard, O.S.B., Review of Anderson, Old Testament and Christian Faith on Voegelin's "History and Gnosis", New Blackfriars, LI (1970), 201.

J. Jensen, O.S.B., Review of Anderson, Old Testament and Christian Faith on Voegelin's "History and Gnosis", American Ecclesiastical Review, CLXIX (1970), 360.

2.   Articles and Essays on Voegelin

Anon, "Journalism and Joachim's Children," Time LXI:10 (1953).

Alois Dempf, et al., Politische Ordnung und menschliche Existenz: Festgabe fuer Eric Voegelin zum 60 Geburtstag, Munich, Beck, 1962.

William C. Harvard, "The Method and Results of Philosophical Anthropology in America," Archiv fuer Rechts- und Sozialphilosophie, LVII (1961), 395-415.

E. Sandoz, "Voegelin's Idea of Historical Form," Cross Currents, XII (1962), 41-63.

D. Germino, "Eric Voegelin's Contribution to Contemporary Political Theory," Review of Politics, XXVI (1964), 378-402. Republished in Beyond Ideology, New York, Harper and Row, 1967, 158-180.

Page Smith, "Spengler, Toynbee and Voegelin," in <u>The</u> <u>Historian</u> <u>and</u> <u>History</u>, New York, Knopf, 1964, 98-109.

G. Niemeyer, "Eric Voegelin's Achievement," <u>Modern</u> <u>Age</u>, XI (1965), 132-140.

Anselm Atkins, "Eric Voegelin and the Decline of Tragedy," <u>Drama</u> <u>Survey</u>, V (1966), 280-285.

Gregor Sebba, "Order and Disorders of the Soul: Eric Voegelin's Philosophy of History," <u>Southern</u> <u>Review</u>, III (1967), 282-310.

Gregor Sebba, "The Present State of Political Theory," <u>Polity</u>, I (1968), 259-270.

Ellis Sandoz, "The Science & The Demonology of Politics, <u>Intercollegiate</u> <u>Review</u>, III (1968), 117-23.

Russell Kirk, "Eric Voegelin's Normative Labor," in <u>Enemies</u> <u>of</u> <u>Permanent</u> <u>Things</u>, New Rochelle, Arlington House, 1969, 253-81.

Ellis Sandoz, "Eric Voegelin and the Nature of Philosophy," <u>The</u> <u>Modern</u> <u>Age</u>, XIII (1969), 152-168.

Malcolm Byrnes, "Toward the Source of Order: An Analysis of Gnosis as the Symbolic Form of Western Political Consciousness in the Work of Eric Voegelin," Ph.D. Thesis, Tulane (1970).

M. Murray, <u>Modern</u> <u>Philosophies</u> <u>of</u> <u>History</u>, The Hague, Martinus Nijhoff, 1970.

John Carmody, "Plato's Religious Horizon" (an application of Voegelin's hermeneutical principles), <u>Philosophy</u> <u>Today</u>, XV (1971), 52-68.

William C. Havard, "Changing Patterns of Voegelin's Conceptions of History and Consciousness," <u>Southern</u> <u>Review</u>, VII (1971), 49-67.

John Kirby, "The Philosophy of the Soul in Eric Voegelin's Order and History (I-III)," M.A. thesis, St. Michael's College, Institute of Christian Thought, University of Toronto, 1972.

J.H. Hallowell "Existence in Tension: Man in Search of His Humanity," Political Science Reviewer, II (1972), 162-184.

S. McKnight, Cassirer, Toynbee and Voegelin on the Intelligible Unity of History, Ph.D. Dissertation, Emory University, 1972.

Ellis Sandoz, "The Philosophical Science of Politics Beyond Behavioralism," in George J. Graham, Jr., and George W. Carey, eds., The Post-Behavioural Era: Perspectives on Political Science, New York, David McKay and Company, 1972, 285-305.

Walter B. Mead, "Restructuring Reality: Signs of the Times." Review of Politics, XXXIV (1972), 342-66.

Eugene Miller, "Positivism, Historicism, and Political Inquiry," American Political Science Review, LXVI (1972), 816.

A.P. D'Entreves "Obbligo Politico e Societa Aperta," Rivista internazionale di Filosofia del Dritto, LIX (1973), 765-70.

Walter B. Mead, "Christian Ambiguity and Social Disorder," Interpretation, III (1973), 221-42.

Ellis Sandoz, "Voegelin Read Anew: Political Philsophy in the Age of Ideology," Modern Age, XVII (1973), 257-263.

Peter J. Opitz, "Autorenportraet: Eric Voegelin," Criticon: Konservative Zeitschrift, XIX (Sept.-Oct., 1973), 200-204.

James L. Wiser, "Political Theory, Personal Knowledge, and Public Truth," Journal of Politics, XXXVI (1974), 661-74

John William Corrington, "A Symposium on Eric Voegelin," Denver Quarterly, X (1975), 93-5.

J.M. Porter, "A Philosophy of History as a Philosophy of Consciousness," Denver Quarterly, X (1975), 96-X4.

James Wiser, "Eric Voegelin and The Eclipse of Philosophy," Denver Quarterly X (1975), 108-114.

John W. Corrington, "Order and History: The Breaking of the Problem," Denver Quarterly, X (1975), 115-22.

William Harvard, "Voegelin's Diagnosis of the Western Crisis," Denver Quarterly, X (1975), 127-34.

Stephen A. McKnight, "Recent Developments in Voegelin's Philosophy of History," Sociological Analysis, XXXVI (1975), 357-365.

John Kirby, "Symbolism and Dogmatism: Voegelin's Distinction," The Ecumenist, XII:2 (Jan. 1975), 26-31.

Dante Germino, "Eric Voegelin: The In-Between of Human Life" in A. De Crespigny and K. Minogue, eds., Contemporary Political Philosophers, New York, Dodd, Mead and Co., 1975, 100-119.

George H. Nash, The Conservative Intellectual Movement in America Since 1945, New York, Basic Books 1976.

Zylstra, Bernard, "Voegelin on Unbelief and Revolution," Antirevolutionaere Staatskunde XLVI (1976), 155-65.

Michael Dillon, "Symbolization and the Search for Order," Intercollegiate Review, XI:2 (1976), 103-11.

Bruce Douglass, "The Gospel & Political Order: Eric Voegelin on the Political Role of Christianity," Journal of Politics, XXXVIII (1976), 25-45.

Stephen A. McKnight, "Voegelin on the Modern Intellectual and Political Crisis," Sociological Analysis, XXXVII (1976), 265-71.

Gerhardt Niemeyer, "Eric Voegelin's Philosophy and The Drama of Mankind," Modern Age, XX (1976), 28-39.

Gregor Sebba, "Prelude and Variations on the Theme of Eric Voegelin," Southern Review, XIII (1977), 646-76.

Barry Cooper, "Voegelin's Concept of Historiogenesis: An Introduction," Historical Reflections/reflexions historiques IV:2 (1977), 231-51.

William Havard, "Notes on Voegelin's Contribution to Political Theory," Polity, X:1 (1977), 33-64.

Douglas Sturm, "Politics & Divinity: Three Approaches in American Political Thought," Thought, LII (1977), 333-65.

Bernard J.F. Lonergan, "Theology and Praxis," Proceedings of the Catholic Theological Society of America, XXXII (1977), 1-16.

Cleanth Brooks, "Walker Percy and Modern Gnosticism," Southern Review, XII (1977), 677-87. Revised version in The Art of Walter Percy: Stratagems for Being, ed., Pantheia Reid Broughton, Baton Rouge, Louisiana State University Press, 1979, 260-72.

Marion Montgomery, "The Poet and the Disquieting Shadow of Being: Flannery O'Connor's Voegelinian Dimension," Intercollegiate Review, XIII:2 (1977), 3-14.

Glen Schram, "Eric Voegelin, Christian Faith, and the American University," Dialog, XVI (1977), 130-35.

Eugene Webb, "Eric Voegelin's Interpretation of Revelation," The Thomist, XLII:1 (1978), 95-122.

John P. East, "Eric Voegelin and American Conservative Thought," Modern Age, XXII (1978), 114-32.

Marion Montgomery, "Flannery O'Connor, Eric Voegelin, and the Question that Lies Between Them," Modern Age, XXII (1978), 133-43.

Harold L. Weatherby, "Myth, Fact, & History: Voegelin on Christianity," Modern Age, XXII (1978), 144-50.

Eric H. Wainwright, "Eric Voegelin: An Inquiry into The Philosophy of Order," Politikon V:1 (1978).

Frederick D. Wilhelmsen, "Eric Voegelin and the Christian Tradition, Christianity and Political Philosophy, Athens, University of Georgia Press, 1978, 193-208.

Eric Harold Wainwright, "The Zetema of Eric Voegelin: Symbol and Experience in Political Reality," Ph.D. thesis, University of South Africa, 1978.

Stephen A. McKnight, ed., Eric Voegelin's Search for Order in History, Baton Rouge, Louisiana State

University Press, 1978. This volume reprinted the following articles: William Havard, "The Changing Pattern of Voegelin's Conception of History and Consciousness" Southern Review, N.S., 7 (1971), 49-67 (some revisions and slight expansion); Bernard Anderson, "Politics and the Transcendent," Political Science Reviewer I (1971), 1-29; John H. Hallowell, "Existence in Tension: Man's Search for His Humanity," Political Science Reviewer, II (1972), 162-84; Hans Aufricht, "A Restatement of Political Theory", Western Political Quarterly, 6 (1953), 448-68. It also contains original essays: Stephen A. McKnight, "The Evolution of Voegelin's Theory of Politics and History, 1944-1975," 26-45; James L. Wiser, "Philosophy as Inquiry and Persuasion," 127-38; Bruce Douglass, "A Diminished Gospel: A Critique of Voegelin's Interpretation of Christianity," 139-54; John William Corrington, "Order and Consciousness, Consciousness & History: The New Program of Voegelin," 155-196.

Ken Kealman, "The Noetic Structure of the Psyche in the Theory of Consciousness in Eric Voegelin," Ph.D Thesis, St. Michael's College, Institute of Christian Thought, University of Toronto, 1979.

Russell Nieli, "From Myth to Philosophy: Eric Voegelin's Theory of Experience and Symbolization," Ph.D. Thesis, Princeton. (1979)

John Kirby, "The Divine and the Human in Voegelin's 'What is Political Reality?'" Ph.D. Thesis, St. Michael's College, Institute of Christian Thought, University of Toronto, 1980.

INDEX

TORONTO STUDIES IN THEOLOGY

DATE DUE
